Controversies in Sociology
edited by
Professor T. B. Bottomore and
Professor M. J. Mulkay

17
Theories of Modern Capitalism

Controversies in Sociology

Theories of
Modern Capitalism

TOM BOTTOMORE

London
George Allen & Unwin
Boston   Sydney

**George Allen & Unwin (Publishers) Ltd,
40 Museum Street, London WC1A 1LU, UK**

George Allen & Unwin (Publishers) Ltd,
Park Lane, Hemel Hempstead, Herts, HP2 4TE, UK

Allen & Unwin, Inc.,
Fifty Cross Street, Winchester, Mass. 01890, USA

George Allen & Unwin Australia Pty Ltd,
8 Napier Street, North Sydney, NSW 2060, Australia

First published in 1985

British Library Cataloguing in Publication Data

Bottomore, Tom
    Theories of modern capitalism.—(Controversies
in sociology; 17)
1. Capitalism
I.Title   II.Series
330.12'2   HB501
ISBN 0–04–301185–3
ISBN 0–04–301186–1 Pbk

Set in 10 on 12 point Times by Ann Buchan (Typesetters), Surrey
and printed in Great Britain
by Biddles Ltd, Guildford, Surrey

Contents

References to works cited in the text and notes are generally given by author and date, with full details of publication provided in the Bibliography at the end of the volume. In the case of works by Marx and Weber, and a few other writings, the original date of publication is given, but where page references are indicated these relate to the English translations, or to later editions, as listed in the Bibliography. I have made my own translation of most of the passages cited from Marx, and have revised the translation of some of those from Weber.

TBB

Theories of Modern Capitalism

Introduction

The debate about the nature and development of modern capitalism begins with Marx's theory of the capitalist mode of production, and of the form of society created by it, which Marx himself usually referred to as 'bourgeois society'.[1] When Marx's ideas began to make their way into European social thought, and into political struggles, in the last two decades of the nineteenth century, they were first critically examined and then, in due course, countered with alternative conceptions of capitalist society. Increasingly, however, his economic theory was ignored – treated, as Joan Robinson has remarked, 'with contemptuous silence, broken only by an occasional mocking footnote' (Robinson, 1942, p. v) – and it was for the most part sociologists, political scientists and historians who continued to pay attention to his ideas and to be influenced by them. One important aspect of this exclusion of Marxist thought from the mainstream of economic theory was the transformation of classical 'political economy' into 'economics' about a century ago, during a phase when, as Hutchinson has observed, 'the interconnections and interdependencies of economics and politics were at an all-time low [and] the political and social framework of the economy . . . . seemed *comparatively* stable' (Hutchinson, 1981, p. vi).

Since that time, and especially since the First World War, the political and social framework has become much more *unstable*, and there has been a rapid growth of state intervention in the economy, with the consequence that political economy (or what economists are more inclined to call macroeconomics) has enjoyed a notable revival, one of its most prominent features being the renaissance of Marxist economic theory. Kühne (1979), in the most elaborate study so far of the relation between Marxist and 'academic' economics, 'sets out to demonstrate three things': first, 'that it was Marx who created the basis for modern macroeconomic theory'; second, 'that Marx was not simply a precursor of all these different theories, but laid the foundations for a continuous development of his own concepts';[2]

and, third, 'that despite his reticence on the future of socialist society, Marx in the *Grundrisse* did at least sketch the transformation of the social system as far as the era of automation' (pp. 4–5).

Marx's theory of capitalism, however, clearly went beyond a purely economic analysis, and even beyond what could be adequately encompassed by the term 'political economy'. It was, in fact, a broad socio-historical theory which treated capitalism as a 'total society', involved in a distinctive process of development. Similarly, the major alternative theories have dealt with capitalism as a distinct form of society in which there are interrelations and interactions between the economy, political and other social institutions, and the cultural sphere.

In the present book, after expounding Marx's conception of capitalism and its 'law of motion', I shall consider some of the rival views of its main characteristics and tendencies, and in particular those of Max Weber, Schumpeter and Hayek. Their ideas introduce into the discussion of capitalism other considerations – about its rationality, its dynamism, or its connection with individual freedom – which may be seen as qualifying, or in some respects replacing, the main structure of Marx's theory; or on the other hand, as being assimilable to it or refutable by it.

Following this critical assessment of the competing paradigms I shall turn, in the last two chapters, to a consideration of the divergent conclusions which have been derived concerning the developmental tendencies of capitalism in its most recent phase, and the possibility, or likelihood, that a different social order, or what Gramsci called 'a new civilization', will emerge from it. The exploration of these questions requires, on one side, a study of the changes in capitalism during the twentieth century and an evaluation of the concepts – 'organized capitalism', 'monopoly capitalism', 'state monopoly capitalism' – that Marxists have used to characterize its present form; on the other side, an analysis of the opposing forces within capitalism and their capacity to bring about a transition to socialism.

My aim, in these concluding chapters, is to present some of the main elements in a '*real* analysis of the inherent nature of present-day capitalism', which Lukács (1971) saw as a major task, though in his view one that 'Marxism has failed to realise so far' (p. vii). The discussion in the final chapter, concerning a transition to socialism, raises many issues which cannot be fully examined within the limits of the present book. I confine myself here to a study of those social conditions and tendencies in the advanced capitalist countries which make possible the creation of a socialist form of society, and leave aside, for the most part, the complex problems of the nature of that socialist 'form' itself – problems which emerge, in large measure, from the experience of 'actually existing socialism', in Eastern Europe, in China and elsewhere.[3]

NOTES TO INTRODUCTION

1 Marx did not use the term 'capitalism' before the late 1870s, in correspondence with his Russian followers about whether Russia could by-pass the capitalist stage of development. In any case the term was not widely used until the latter part of the nineteenth century; the *Oxford English Dictionary* indicates the first reference to 'capitalism' (by Thackeray) as being in 1854.

2 In this context he cites Bronfenbrenner's (1965) summary: 'Marx's theoretical economic system . . . . may be regarded as a system of moving equilibrium at less than full employment. In this respect it anticipates Keynes. It also goes beyond Keynes, in deriving an employment position which deteriorates over time . . . . This level will eventually become impossible to maintain . . . . This is the dilemma which drives the system to stagnation and eventual breakdown . . . . This dilemma is at once an economic "contradiction of capitalism" and the "law of motion" of the capitalist economy . . . .' (p. 206).

3 These questions will be examined directly in another work, which is complementary to the present study: Tom Bottomore, *The Socialist Economy in Theory and Practice* (Brighton: Harvester Press, forthcoming).

1
Marx's Theory of the Commodity-Producing Society

Marx's theory of modern capitalism was constructed in several stages as part of a more general theory of society. The first stage was that in which Marx, during 1842–3, formed his conception of the proletariat as a distinctive element, and a major political force, in the new type of society that was coming into existence in Western Europe. But the proletariat, as Marx noted, was a product of the industrial movement, and in order to understand fully its social situation and historical significance it would be necessary to study in detail the economic structure and development of the modern Western societies. Hence, in a second stage of his work, and guided initially by the studies which Engels had already devoted to political economy,[1] Marx embarked upon an extensive reading of the economists – in particular, Say, James Mill, List, Adam Smith and Ricardo – and filled a series of notebooks with critical comments on their writings.

The first results of these economic studies were set down in the *Economic and Philosophical Manuscripts* (1844), where Marx formulated a broad conception of human labour as being not only the source of material wealth – and therefore the basis of all social life – but also the means through which the human species develops its specifically human qualities and constructs particular forms of society. The distinctive nature of capitalist society, as one of these forms, is then outlined in the following terms:

Labour does not only create goods; it also produces itself and the worker as a *commodity*, and indeed in the same proportion as it produces goods. This fact simply implies that the object produced by labour, its product, now stands opposed to it as an *alien being*, as a *power independent* of the producer . . . .

The third stage in the formation of Marx's thought was the incorporation of his conception of labour into a systematic theory of the historical development of human society. This was accomplished in various writings of the mid-1840s, and notably in the manuscripts of *The German Ideology* (1845–6) where Marx summarized his view as follows:

This conception of history, therefore, rests on the exposition of the real process of production, starting out from the simple material production of life, and on the comprehension of the form of intercourse connected with and created by this mode of production, i.e. of civil society in its various stages as the basis of all history, and also in its action as the state. From this starting point, it explains all the different theoretical productions and forms of consciousness, religion, philosophy, ethics, etc., and traces their origins and growth, by which means the matter can of course be displayed as a whole (and consequently also the reciprocal action of these various sides on one another). (*German Ideology*, Vol. 1, s. 1A,2)

Similarly, in a letter to P. V. Annenkov (28 December 1846) he wrote:

What is society, regardless of its particular form? The product of men's interaction. Are men free to choose this or that social form. Not at all. Assume a certain stage of development of men's productive powers and you will have a particular form of commerce and consumption. Assume certain levels of development of production, commerce, and consumption, and you will have a particular type of social constitution, a particular organization of the family, of ranks or classes; in short a particular form of civil society. Assume a determinate form of civil society and you will have a particular type of political regime, which is only the official expression of civil society.

After outlining this new conception of the development of human society – which remained the foundation of his whole social theory, and was restated in the preface to *A Contribution to the Critique of Political Economy* (1859), where 'the Asiatic, the ancient, the feudal, and the modern bourgeois modes of production' were designated as 'progressive epochs in the economic formation of society' – Marx concentrated his main scientific effort, for the rest of his life, upon the analysis of one particular historical form of society: Western capitalism.[2] What distinguishes bourgeois or capitalist society from other types of society is that social production here takes the form of a generalized production of commodities:

> The wealth of those societies in which the capitalist mode of production prevails, appears as 'an immense accumulation of commodities', with the individual commodity as its elementary unit. Our investigation therefore begins with an analysis of the commodity. (*Capital*, Vol. 1, ch. 1)

First, Marx distinguishes the 'two factors of a commodity': use value (i.e. those qualities which satisfy some human want), and value (which manifests itself in the form of exchange value, i.e. the proportion in which use values of one kind are exchanged for use values of another kind, this proportion being expressed in a developed capitalist economy in terms of the 'general equivalent', money). He then proceeds to analyse 'the dual character of the labour embodied in commodities', which corresponds with these two factors: (i) the specific, qualitatively distinct, kinds of useful labour which produce particular use values, and (ii) abstract labour, or 'human labour pure and simple, the expenditure of human labour power in general', which creates the value of commodities. It is the conjunction in the commodity of use value and value, useful and abstract labour, that accounts for its 'enigmatic character', or what Marx goes on to call the 'fetishism of commodities'; which consists in the fact that the commodity form presents the social character of labour as 'an objective characteristic of the products of labour themselves', so that 'the social relation of the producers to the sum total of their own labour appears to them as a social relation between objects'. But this is a necessary appearance, a real phenomenon in capitalist society; for useful objects only become commodities because they are the products of independently producing private individuals or groups, the social character of whose individual labour only manifests itself when exchange takes place.

Marx's intention was to reveal the specific form of the social labour process in a capitalist society, as may be seen very clearly from a note on his theory of value which he wrote towards the end of his life: '. . . . the "value" of the commodity only expresses in a historically developed form what also exists in all other historical forms of society, even though *in another form; namely, the social character of labour*, in so far as it exists as the *expenditure of "social" labour power'.*[3] But Marx's analysis of capitalism was not only guided in this way by his conception of historical stages of development; it was also based upon other elements in his general social theory, and notably the theory of classes. For Marx, capitalism was only one of the forms of class society, which he characterized in general terms as follows:

The specific economic form in which unpaid surplus labour is pumped out of the direct producers determines the relation of domination and servitude, as it emerges directly out of production itself and in its turn reacts upon production . . . . It is always the direct relation between the owners of the conditions of production and the direct producers which reveals the innermost secret, the hidden foundation of the entire social edifice, and therefore also of the political form of the relation between sovereignty and dependence, in short, of the particular form of the state. The form of this relation between owners and producers always necessarily corresponds to a definite stage in the development of the methods of work and consequently of the social productivity of labour. (*Capital*, Vol. 1, ch. 47)

The analysis of capitalism has therefore to be pursued further, in order to show, with respect to this specific form of society, precisely how unpaid surplus labour is pumped out of the direct producers;[4] and Marx proceeds to argue that in capitalist society labour power itself becomes a commodity, but one which has the unique property of being able to add more value to other commodities, when it is expended in production, than its own value, which is determined (in a manner similar to that of any other commodity)[5] by the abstract labour socially necessary for its maintenance and reproduction. This peculiarity of labour power as a commodity Marx summarizes in his conception of 'necessary' and 'surplus' labour, the former being that which broadly maintains the aggregate sum of labour power (though the required sum may fluctuate), the latter being the source of 'surplus value' which is appropriated by the owners of the conditions (or means) of production and is partly consumed by them, partly accumulated as capital.

From this analysis there also appears another distinctive feature of capitalism; namely, that the extraction of surplus labour (for which Marx uses the term 'exploitation' as a technical expression) here takes place as a more or less purely economic process, whereas in earlier forms of society, based upon the labour of slaves or serfs, it required some kind of extra-economic compulsion. But this also means that exploitation is less apparent; for, while the slave or serf experiences directly the fact that a part of the product of his labour is appropriated by a dominant group, the wage-worker is engaged in a process of production in which he/she apparently exchanges labour for other commodities (via the wage) at its real value, and the mechanism by which a surplus product is generated and appropriated is obscured.[6] Hence the need, according to Marx, for a scientific analysis of the capitalist economy in order to reveal, beneath the surface appearance, its fundamental structure and mode of operation, and the crucial importance in such an analysis of the distinction between 'labour' and 'labour power'.

Marx's model of the basic elements of a 'purely capitalist society'[7] was not the conclusion of his theory, but the starting point for a comprehensive study of the real historical development of modern capitalism. This involved examining, in particular, the development of production by machinery (machinofacture), the centralization and concentration of capital, economic crises, and the evolution of class conflict.

Marx regarded the advent of machinofacture (including the production of machines by machines) as marking the mature phase of the capitalist mode of production in which there is a 'real subsumption of labour under capital';[8] that is, the dominance of machinery in the labour process, incessant transformation of the labour process, and the imposition of strict factory discipline, so that the worker becomes 'a living appendage' of the lifeless machine and 'it is not the worker who employs the means of labour, but on the contrary, the means of labour employ the worker' (*Capital*, Vol. 1, ch. 13). Two factors determine the development of machinofacture. One, evidently, is the progress of technology (i.e. the industrial revolution) based upon science, which Marx continually emphasizes, in conformity with his general view of the determining influence of the forces of production in the historical process. From this aspect capitalism is described in glowing terms as an immense advance in human productive powers:

> The bourgeoisie, during its rule of scarce one hundred years, has created more massive and more colossal productive powers than have all preceding generations together. Subjection of nature's forces to man, machinery, application of chemistry to industry and agriculture, steam navigation, railways, electric telegraphs, clearing of whole continents for cultivation, canalization of rivers, whole populations conjured out of the ground – what earlier century had even a presentiment that such productive forces slumbered in the lap of social labour? (*Communist Manifesto*, s. 1)

What Marx emphasizes particularly in his analysis of machinofacture is its basis in the growth of scientific knowledge, and its influence in extending and making more evident the social character of labour; there develop, he says

> on an ever-extending scale, the co-operative form of the labour process, the conscious application of science, the

planned exploitation of the earth, the transformation of the instruments of labour into instruments which can only be used in co-operative work, the economizing of all means of production by their use as the means of production of combined, socialized labour, the entanglement of all peoples in the net of the world market, and with this, the international character of the capitalist system. (*Capital*, Vol. 1, ch. 24)

These ideas, as we shall see, play an important part in Marx's analysis of the later phases of capitalist development, and of the transition to socialism.

The second factor in the extension of production by machinery is the competition among capitalists. In elaborating his theory of capitalism Marx proceeds from an analysis of capital in general to a study of the empirical phenomena of capitalist production, in which many individual capitals compete with each other. In this competition the use of machinery plays a major part, for it is through the continual improvement of machinery that the productivity of labour, and hence the rate and/or mass of surplus value accruing to the individual capitalist producer, can be increased. Hence the progress of technology, which is a necessary condition for the development of machinofacture, comes in turn to be powerfully influenced by capitalist competition. On one side there is a relatively independent growth of science and technology; on the other, an immense stimulus to technological innovation arising from the desire of individual capitalist producers to raise productivity and so increase the mass of surplus value available for accumulation and the self-expansion of capital.

But machinofacture also has another socio-economic effect, on the concentration of capital. Marx distinguishes in the phenomenon of concentration two separate processes. One, which he calls 'concentration', is the growth of the mass of capital (in general or in the hands of an individual capitalist) through the accumulation of surplus value, i.e. the reinvestment of profits in new means of production. The second, which he calls 'centralization', is the absorption of weaker capitalists by those who are stronger, brought about by competition. In Marx's words 'One capitalist always kills many'. This latter process, which leads towards the domination of production by giant firms (in the form of joint-stock companies or corporations), to oligopoly and monopoly, is stimulated by the growth of machinofacture, for the constant revolutionizing of methods of production through the introduction of ever more sophisticated and expensive machinery requires on one side the investment of vast amounts of capital and on the other side a vast output and sale of products if the benefits of large-scale production by machinery, in the form of a greater mass of profits, are to be achieved.

The two aspects of Marx's theory of capitalist development which I have so far considered – the fundamental importance of technological progress and the powerful underlying tendency to increase the scale of production – are those which have received the most favourable attention in recent times from non-Marxist economists, and as will be seen in a later chapter they provide a significant point of contact between the ideas of Schumpeter and Marx. A third element in Marx's theory – his analysis of economic crises – is, by contrast, less fully elaborated and far more contentious. That part of his 'Economics' (outlined in the Introduction to the *Grundrisse*) which was to have been devoted to 'the world market and crises' was never written, and later Marxists have been obliged to construct a theory of crises for themselves on the basis of diverse comments and arguments which are dispersed through Marx's writings,[9] with the consequence that different, sometimes conflicting, theories have been propounded.[10] One is an underconsumption theory, which has its source in Marx's comment in *Capital* (Vol. 3, ch. 30) that 'the ultimate cause of all real crises is always the poverty and restricted consumption of the masses, in contrast with the tendency of capitalist production to develop the productive forces as though only the absolute consuming power of society constituted their limit', and also to some extent in his discussion of 'luxury consumption' (*Capital*, Vol. 2, ch. 20). But although there are underconsumptionist elements in several Marxist theories (e.g., those of Luxemburg and Sweezy) any simple underconsumption view has been generally rejected as inconsistent with the broader framework of Marx's approach.[11]

A second theory is that which concentrates upon the 'ten-year cycle of modern industry' (see *Capital*, Vol. 2, ch. 20, and the discussion in Kühne 1979, Vol. 2, ch. 14) – and discerns a major cause of crises in the emergence of distortions and overcapacity during the boom,[12] followed by hoarding of money and accumulation of stocks. This conception is related to another theory of crises – the 'disproportionality' theory – which was most fully developed by Hilferding (1910, part 4). According to this view crises occur as a result of disproportionate growth in different branches of production (and in particular dispropor- tions between the two departments which produce investment goods and consumer goods respectively); and Hilferding emphasizes the difficulty of maintaining 'the complicated relations of proportionality which must exist in production', given the 'anarchic character' of the capitalist economy and the incessant transformations brought about by technological progress, population increase and other factors. This difficulty has been strongly emphasized again in some recent Marxist writing; thus Harvey (1982) argues that Marx posed as a basic question:

. . . . how can the processes of technological and organiza- tional change, as regulated by individual capitalists acting under the class relations of capitalism, ever achieve the viable technology to permit balanced accumulation and the repro- duction of class relations in perpetuity? . . . . he [Marx] makes a pretty good case that the necessary technological and organizational mix could only ever be struck temporarily by accident and that the behaviour of individual capitalists tends perpetually to de-stabilize the economic system. (p. 189)

One important element in Hilferding's account of the causes of crises was the 'tendency of the rate of profit to fall' (expounded by Marx, together with a discussion of the 'counteracting influences', in *Capital*, Vol, 3, part 3), and in the work of some recent Marxists this has been elaborated as a further, distinctive theory of crises. Thus Fine and Harris (1979) argue that the main cause of crises (defined as 'forcible changes in the progress of capitalist accumulation') is the contradictory development of the tendency of the rate of profit to fall and the counteracting influences.[13] They then proceed from an abstract analysis in terms of values to consider how various observable phenomena – hoarding, restriction or collapse of the credit system, class struggle and the competitive determination of wages, the relations between the financial and industrial bourgeoisie – are founded upon the determining contradictions (pp. 84–5). Finally, they examine how the state, in advanced capitalist societies, intervenes to affect the course of the cycle (the restructuring of productive capital), not only by direct economic means but also ideologically and politically, especially by reducing expenditure on welfare services and strengthening the capitalistic element in nationalised industries.

Whether there is now emerging a more systematic Marxist theory of crises, and a wider consensus upon its principal components, may be debatable,[14] but some important aspects of it at least are now clear. First, it is evident that Marx's own theory 'is not presented . . . . in an easily accessible form' (Fine and Harris, 1979, p. 80), or more strongly expressed, that 'Marx left us with several partial analyses but no picture of the totality' (Harvey, 1982, p. 79). In particular, it should be noted that Marx analysed only short-term cycles of about ten years and did not concern himself at all with any longer cycles (such as the 'long waves' suggested later by van Gelderen and Kondratiev) which, so far as their occurrence is adequately established, need to be taken into account in any comprehensive theory of economic crises. It is only recently that some Marxists – notably Mandel[15] – have again given serious attention to such phenomena.

A more important aspect is that none of Marx's partial analyses embody a conception of crises as leading to an ineluctable 'economic breakdown' of capitalism, such as some later Marxists (e.g., Grossmann) formulated,[16] although it is occasionally suggested that economic crises will become progressively more intense, and 'by their periodical return put the existence of the entire bourgeois society on its trial, each time more threateningly' (*Communist Manifesto*, s. 1). On the contrary, Marx's general view seems to have been that crises, in purely economic terms, are a means of countering disequilibrium and re-establishing the conditions for further capitalist development:

From time to time the conflict of antagonistic agencies gives
vent to crises. The crises are always only momentary and
forcible solutions of the existing contradictions, violent
eruptions which for a time restore the disturbed equilibrium.
(*Capital*, Vol. 3, ch. 15)[17]

From the standpoint of Marx's general social theory the
question of the ultimate demise of capitalism and a transition to
socialism has to be examined in the broader context of the
conflict between classes, as Hilferding (1910) saw clearly when
he interpreted Marxist thought as signifying that 'the collapse of
capitalism will be political and social, not economic', and went on
to consider the new circumstances of working-class struggle in
the era of 'finance capital'.[18] The concepts of class and class
struggle have a place of fundamental importance in Marx's
analysis of capitalist society and its development; but his theory
of classes was even less fully and systematically elaborated than
was his theory of economic crises, and in this case too later
Marxists have been obliged to construct theoretical schemes for
themselves. This has led to diverse interpretations of Marx's
thought, compounded by the need to take account of the changes
in capitalism during the century since Marx's death, and the
emergence of a great range of new political phenomena – among
them fascism, Bolshevism, the consequences of two world wars,
the division of the world between superpowers, the implications
of the tremendous scientific and technological revolution in
which humanity is now involved.

The question to be considered here, deferring to a later
chapter (Chapter 6) a discussion of those issues which concern
specifically the conditions for a transition to socialism, is whether
we can derive from Marx's work a clear conception of the
'phases' of capitalist development which lead towards its
eventual transformation and supersession. Marx, it is evident,
regarded capitalism as a historically transient form of society,
and mocked the economists who treated the relations of
bourgeois production as 'natural laws, independent of the
influence of time':

Thus there has been history, but there is no longer any history.

There has been history, because there were feudal institutions, and because in these feudal institutions are to be found relations of production entirely different from those in bourgeois society, which latter none the less the economists wish to present as natural and therefore eternal. (*Poverty of Philosophy*, ch. 2, s. 1, 'Seventh and last observation')

But he did not argue that capitalism would disappear simply because previous forms of society had done so, as the outcome of some mysterious teleological process.[19] He undertook rather to analyse the real contradictions of capitalist society – the antagonistic forces at work within it – which might be expected to bring about its decline and the emergence of a new form of society.

These antagonistic forces are embodied, according to Marx's conception, in the class struggle between bourgeoisie and proletariat, and the idea of widening and intensifying conflict is to be found in many texts: in the *Communist Manifesto*, where it is argued that 'society is more and more splitting up into two great hostile camps'; in the *Poverty of Philosophy*, where the formation of the proletariat as a 'class for itself', engaged in a political struggle, is sketched; and in a well-known passage of *Capital* (Vol. 1, ch. 24), which describes how 'along with the constantly diminishing number of magnates of capital . . . . grows the mass of misery, oppression, slavery, degradation, exploitation; but with this too grows the revolt of the working class, a class always increasing in numbers, and disciplined, united, organized by the mechanism of the capitalist production process itself'.

Elsewhere, however, Marx recognizes a greater complexity of the class structure, and even a different course of development. In the fragment on classes at the end of *Capital* (Vol. 3) he observes that even in England 'intermediate and transitional strata obscure the class boundaries', and in *Theories of Surplus Value* (ch. 17, s. 6), in the course of discussing economic crises, he notes that he is disregarding for the purpose of his preliminary analysis 'the real constitution of society, which by no means consists only of the class of workers and the class of industrial capitalists'. Still more significantly, in two other comments in

Theories of Surplus Value he refers to the growth of the middle classes:

> What [Ricardo] forgets to emphasize is the continual increase in numbers of the middle classes . . . . situated midway between the workers on one side and the capitalists and landowners on the other . . . . [who] rest with all their weight upon the working basis and at the same time increase the social security and power of the upper ten thousand. (ch. 18, s. B1d)

And again (with reference to Malthus):

> his greatest hope . . . . is that the middle class will increase in size and the working proletariat will make up a constantly diminishing proportion of the total population (even if it grows in absolute numbers). That is, in fact, the tendency of bourgeois society. (ch. 19, s. 14)

Since Marx never completed (indeed scarcely began) that part of his work which was intended to analyse class relations in capitalist society, it is impossible to know how he would have brought together, in a rigorous theoretical scheme, his divergent observations on the class structure, or precisely how he conceived its further development and the consequences this might have for political struggles. In any case, we need to pay attention not only to Marx's own scattered and unsystematic observations, but also to the actual development of classes and class struggles in the century since his death. This, however, is an issue of the utmost complexity, around which very diverse historical interpretations and intense controversies have accumulated.[20] Perhaps as a preliminary approach to the problem (to be elaborated more fully in Chapter 5 below) it may be suggested that Marx's notion of the increasing polarization of society and the growing intensity of class conflict should be seen as the formulation of a 'tendency' whose working out in practice is inhibited by various 'counter-tendencies'. This would be to adopt the kind of model that Marx indicated in his discussion of the 'tendency of the rate of profit to fall', and in the case of an analysis of class struggles would involve setting against the historical development, since the latter part of the nineteenth century, of class-based political parties and movements those countervailing tendencies (ranging from the expansion of the middle class to the massive growth of productive powers and the extension of social services) which have, for the most part, and in particular since 1945, prevented any major confrontations between classes.

But we must now also consider the second way in which Marx conceives the development of capitalism; namely, as a process of increasing socialization of the economy. In *Capital* (Vol. 3, ch. 15) he summarizes the 'three principal aspects of capitalist production' as follows:

1   The concentration of means of production into a few hands, as a result of which they are no longer the property of the direct producers but are transformed into social powers of production . . . .
2   The organization of labour itself as social labour, by co-operation, division of labour, and the union of labour with the natural sciences.

   From both sides the capitalist mode of production abolishes private property and private (individual) labour, though it does so in an antagonistic form.
3   The creation of a world market.

Later in the same work (ch. 23) Marx discusses the significance of the development of joint-stock companies, which 'have a tendency to separate the function of management more and more from the ownership of capital, whether it be self-owned or borrowed'. In addition:

   . . . . money capital itself assumes a social character with the development of credit, being concentrated in banks and loaned by them instead of by its original owners, while on the other hand the mere manager, who has no title whatever to the capital whether by borrowing or otherwise, performs all the real functions of the investing capitalist as such; only the functionary remains and the capitalist disappears from the process of production as a superfluous person.

This, Marx concludes, 'is the abolition of the capitalist mode of production within capitalist production itself, a self-transcending contradiction which is *prima facie* only a phase of transition to a new form of production . . . . the capitalist joint-stock companies, just as much as the co-operative factories, have to be seen as transitional forms between the capitalist mode of production and the associated one, only that the opposition is transcended negatively in the one and positively in the other' (ibid., ch. 27).

Finally, in the *Grundrisse*, Marx considers the consequences of the rapid progress of science and technology, and the advent of automated production:

But to the extent that large-scale industry develops, the creation of real wealth comes to depend less on labour time and on the amount of labour employed than on the power of the agencies set in motion during labour time, whose 'powerful effectiveness' is in turn out of all proportion to the direct labour time spent on their production, and depends rather on the general state of science and on the progress of technology, or the application of this science to production . . . . In this transformation it is neither the direct labour which the human being himself performs, nor the time during which he works, but rather the appropriation of his own general productive power, his understanding of nature and his mastery over it by virtue of his existence as a social entity – in a word, the development of the social individual – which now appears as the great foundation of production and wealth . . . . The development of fixed capital indicates the extent to which general social knowledge has become a direct force of production, and thus the extent to which the conditions of the social life process have been brought under the control of the general intellect and reconstructed in accordance with it. (Notebook 7, section on 'Contradiction between the basis of bourgeois production and its development', English edition, pp. 704–6)

These texts, while they do not directly contradict Marx's analysis of the development of capitalism in terms of class struggle, do introduce additional (and qualifying) elements by suggesting that a phase of capitalism will eventually be reached in which the social character of the labour process, and of production in general, becomes more clearly recognized in society at large, and is even in some degree consciously reinforced by diverse attempts to regulate and guide the economy as a whole. This is the idea which Hilferding later expressed in his conception of 'organized capitalism'[21] as a stage of capitalist development in which the dominance of large corporations, the growth of state intervention in the economy, and the emergence of various forms of economic planning create the necessary preconditions for transforming 'an economy organized and directed by the capitalists into one which is directed by the democratic state'. The notion of 'organized capitalism' as an advanced stage of socialization of the economy has implanted itself firmly in recent Marxist thought,[22] and, as we shall see, it plays an important part also in Schumpeter's theory. Whether, and in what sense, it can be characterized further as the phase in which a transition to socialism occurs is an issue which I shall examine in the concluding chapter of this book.

Marx's theory of capitalism, as I have outlined it here, left a number of unsettled questions for the attention of later Marxists. The basic elements of the capitalist mode of production – generalized commodity production, labour power as a commodity, extraction of surplus value – were analysed by Marx in considerable detail. So too were the dynamic features of the capitalist system – the driving force being accumulation, determined by the competition among capitalists and depending upon (but also stimulating) the progress of science and technology. But Marx was not able to pursue with anything like the same thoroughness his proposed study of the social and political context of capitalist development – that is to say, to analyse capitalism as a historically evolving total society – and it is in this sphere especially that attempts have been made, since the end of the nineteenth century, to extend his theory. In due course I shall consider some of the principal Marxist analyses of what has been called 'advanced capitalism' or 'late capitalism'.

First, however, it is necessary to examine those alternative theories of capitalism which themselves enter into the debate about the nature and prospects of present-day Western societies.

NOTES TO CHAPTER 1

1 In particular his essay 'Umrisse zu einer Kritik der Nationalökonomie' (Outlines of a critique of political economy), published in the *Deutsch-Französische Jahrbücher*, edited by Marx and Ruge (1844).

2 Though this was clearly intended also as a model for the analysis of other forms of society, and indeed a privileged model, for, as Marx argues in the Introduction to the *Grundrisse*, 'bourgeois economy provides a key to the economy of antiquity' just as there is 'a key to the anatomy of apes in the anatomy of human beings'; but at the same time the 'essential differences' have to be recognized and 'if it is true that the categories of bourgeois economy possess a truth for all other forms of society, that must be taken with a grain of salt', and the categories (e.g. tribute, tithes, ground rent) relevant to different forms of society must not be treated as identical.

3 'Notes on Adolph Wagner's *Manual of Political Economy*', written in 1879–80 and first published in 1930. An English translation, with commentary and notes, is given in Terrell Carver (1975).

4 And beyond that, how the relation between sovereignty and dependence – or the particular form of the state – is determined. Marx never investigated this aspect of capitalist society in a comprehensive or systematic way, and his unfinished reflections on the subject, which have been diversely interpreted, will be discussed later in this chapter.

5 Labour power, however, is a distinctive commodity in several respects, one of them being that it is not produced *as* a commodity; but these complications do not affect the argument in the present context. See the entry 'Labour power' in Tom Bottomore (ed.), *A Dictionary of Marxist Thought* (1983).

6 Marx argued, however, that the origins of capitalism, i.e. the process of 'primitive accumulation', had also required various kinds of violence and physical coercion. 'Capital', he wrote, 'comes into the world oozing blood and filth from every pore' (*Capital*, Vol. 1, ch. 24).

7 For the use of this expression see Kozo Uno (1980).

8 For Marx's distinction between the 'formal' and the 'real' subsumption (or subordination) of labour see his manuscript 'Results of the immediate process of production', first published in 1933; English trans. in *Capital*, Vol. 1, Appendix (Harmondsworth: Penguin, 1976). But the distinction is in any case clearly and comprehensively set out, in other terms, in *Capital*, Vol. 1, ch. 12, 'Division of Labour and Manufacture' and ch. 13, 'Machinery and Large-Scale Industry'.

9 Furthermore, these discussions are to be found mainly in three incomplete and unrevised manuscripts which were only published after Marx's death: *Capital*, Vol. 3 (especially ch. 13–15 and 30), *Theories of Surplus Value*, Vol. 2, ch. 13, and *Grundrisse* (in the sections on overproduction, pp. 414–23 in the Penguin edition).

10 For an account of the alternative views (including assessments by non-Marxist economists) see Karl Kühne, 1979, Vol. 2, part 3; David

Harvey, 1982, especially chs. 3, 6 and 7; B. Fine and L. Harris, 1979, ch. 5; and the entry 'Economic crises' in Bottomore, 1983. See also the comments in J. A. Schumpeter, 1954, pp. 1131–2.

11 Thus Hilferding (1910, p. 241) observed that ' "overproduction of commodities" and "underconsumption" tell us very little', and Schumpeter (1942, pp. 38–9) argued that Marx 'expressly repudiated' a naive underconsumption or overproduction theory 'of the most contemptible type'. Many recent Marxists have similarly rejected this kind of theory.

12 In *Theories of Surplus Value* (Vol. 2, ch. 17) Marx observes that 'the market expands more slowly than production . . . . there comes a moment at which the market manifests itself as too narrow for production'.

13 See also the entry 'Economic crises' in Bottomore, 1983.

14 Mandel, in his contribution to David McLellan, 1983, claims that 'the present "long depression" has not given birth up till now to any significant new development of theoretical analysis, either in Marxist or in non-Marxist circles. Whether this is because the theory of crisis (of business cycles) has already reached a high level of perfection, or whether it is due to an excessive preoccupation with immediate (and pragmatic) analysis, remains to be seen' (p. 211).

15 See Mandel, 1975, ch. 4, ' "Long Waves" in the History of Capitalism'.

16 See the brief account in Kühne, 1979, Vol. 2, ch. 26.

17 In this respect Marx's view has something in common with Schumpeter's conception of 'gales of creative destruction' as an inherent feature of capitalist development, and this will be considered more fully in Chapter 3 below.

18 Hilferding, 1910, chs. 23–5.

19 The criticism of Marx's 'historicism' by Popper (1957) rests on the mistaken assumption that this is his underlying argument.

20 I have discussed it more fully, from various aspects, in Bottomore, 1965, and in a number of essays collected in Bottomore, 1975 and 1984a. See also the valuable study by Abercrombie and Urry, 1983.

21 See Hilferding, 1910, and 'The organized economy' in Bottomore and Goode, 1983.

22 For example, in the discussions of 'state monopoly capitalism'; see Bottomore and Goode, 1983, Part 7, and also Hardach and Karras, 1978, ch. 4.

2

Max Weber on Capitalism and Rationality

A great unifying theme in Max Weber's work, as has been argued in a recent study (Brubaker, 1984), is the idea of rationality, and more particularly the 'specific and peculiar rationalism' which characterizes modern Western civilization.[1] For Weber, the principal manifestation of this rationalism, and of the process of 'rationalization', is modern capitalism, 'the most fateful force in our modern life',[2] although this has to be situated in the context of a wider movement of the rationalization of knowledge (science), religion, law and administration.

In the second chapter of *Economy and Society* (1921) Weber analyses the main features of rational economic action in a capitalist society, and contrasts such action with economic orientations in other forms of society. These features are: exchange in the market ('the archetype of all rational social action', where transactions are determined only by the 'purposeful pursuit of interests'); the generalized use of money, which is the most 'perfect' means of economic accounting, and more specifically, rational capital accounting; the rational organization of labour in production and strict factory discipline; a rational technology; the most complete possible separation of the enterprise from the household. Outside the economic sphere as such it is necessary that there should be complete calculability of the functioning of public administration and the legal order, and a reliable formal guarantee of all contracts by the political authority.

Weber distinguishes (ch. 2, s. 31) between different modes of capitalistic orientation to profit-making, in order to determine the specific characteristics of modern capitalism, and he concludes that 'it is only in the Western world that rational capitalist enterprises with permanent capital, free labour, rational specialization and combination of labour, and the market allocation of productive functions on the basis of profit-making capitalist enterprises, are to be found'. This involves a formally 'voluntary organization of labour', the expropriation of means of production from workers, and the appropriation of enterprises by shareholders. Weber also examines (s. 14) the difference between a 'market economy' and a 'planned economy', partly in order to bring out more clearly the specific character of capitalist rationality, partly as an element in his critical view of the possibility of socialism.

Weber's reflections in *Economy and Society* do not amount to a theory of capitalism; indeed, in his prefatory note to Chapter 2, he observes that:

> What follows is not intended in any sense to be 'economic theory'. Rather, it consists only in an attempt to define certain concepts which are frequently used and to analyse certain of the simplest sociological relationships in the economic sphere.

Furthermore, even a systematic model or 'ideal type' of modern capitalism is not explicitly presented here, but has to be pieced together from diverse analyses of economic relationships in general. A much more comprehensive and coherent view of modern capitalism is to be found in the *General Economic History* (1923), Part 4, which Collins (1980) quite properly treats as the 'mature theory'. In this text Weber begins by stating that:

> Capitalism is present wherever the industrial provision for the needs of a human group is carried out by the method of enterprise, irrespective of what need is involved. (p. 207)

He continues by specifying the basic conditions of a capitalist economy:

> The most general presupposition for the existence of this

present-day capitalism is that of rational capital accounting as the norm for all large industrial undertakings . . . . Such accounting involves, again, first, the appropriation of all physical means of production – land, apparatus, machinery, tools, etc. – as disposable property of autonomous private industrial enterprises . . . . In the second place, it involves freedom of the market, that is, the absence of irrational limitations on trading in the market . . . . Third, capitalistic accounting presupposes rational technology, that is, one reduced to calculation to the largest possible degree, which implies mechanization . . . . The fourth characteristic is that of calculable law . . . . The fifth feature is free labour. Persons must be present who are not only legally in the position, but are also economically compelled, to sell their labour on the market without restriction . . . . The sixth and final condition is the commercialization of economic life. By this we mean the general use of commercial instruments to represent share rights in enterprise, and also in property ownership. (pp. 208–9).

This exposition has several distinctive features. First, Weber here defines capitalism generally in terms of 'the method of enterprise', and attributes a central role to the 'large entrepreneurs' who are 'the creators of the modern economic situation' (p. 264). The significance of the entrepreneur for the development of 'rational capitalism' is later discussed in the context of the emergence of a new economic ethic, and the Calvinist concept of a 'calling', which 'expresses the value placed upon rational activity carried on according to the rational capitalistic principle, as the fulfilment of a God-given task . . . . [and] quickly gave to the modern entrepreneur a fabulously clear conscience – and also industrious workers' (p. 269).[3] Nevertheless, the role of the Protestant ethic in the rise of capitalism is not strongly emphasized and, as Collins (1980) notes, more attention is given to Marxian themes, such as the private ownership of the means of production, the sale of labour power (though Weber ignores Marx's crucial distinction between 'labour' and 'labour power' and refers simply to 'labour'), and the importance of technology.

Where Weber's account of the preconditions for the existence of capitalism diverges most noticeably from Marx (beyond its brief references to the entrepreneur and the influence of a religious ethic) is, first, in its emphasis upon the market rather than the process of production, and, second, in the attention given to the political and legal framework. As Collins (1980) remarks, the main picture is of 'the institutional foundations of the market as viewed by neo-classical economics', or in other words a model or 'ideal type' of a *laissez-faire* capitalist economy. In developing this model Weber discusses first the economic factors in the rise of capitalism (pp. 209–32); then the growth of citizenship, involving the formation of classes with distinct interests, and at the same time membership of a state (pp. 233–49). The formation of national states and the competitive struggle between them created according to Weber:

> The largest opportunities for modern Western capitalism . . . . Out of this alliance of the state with capital, dictated by necessity, arose the national citizen class, the bourgeoisie in the modern sense of the word. Hence it is the closed national state which afforded to capitalism its chance for development. (p. 249)

Furthermore, this national state is also a 'rational state', based upon expert officialdom and rational law, 'in which alone modern capitalism can flourish' (p. 250) because it requires, in this sphere too, a high degree of 'calculability'. Only in the concluding pages of the book (pp. 258–7) does Weber discuss the 'capitalist spirit' and the entrepreneur, whose role, as we shall see, was more fully analysed, and given much greater prominence, by Schumpeter.

In the *General Economic History* Weber is concerned only with the origin of capitalism, not with the 'law of motion' of a fully constituted capitalist society, and in this respect too he differs fundamentally from Marx. Moreover, even in this more restricted study of origins Weber does not propound a theory, in the sense of a causal explanation, but rather distinguishes a variety of circumstances which had to occur together (and actually happened to occur) as prerequisites for the emergence of modern capitalism. This approach is consonant with his general conception of the 'uniqueness' of modern Western society, and with his rejection of a Marxist theory of history as a law-governed process in which the principal causal factors can be clearly specified.

Neither in the *General Economic History*, therefore, nor in *Economy and Society* does Weber treat capitalism as a dynamic form of society which may pass through various stages of development – for example, as a result of inner tensions or contradictions. On one side, he distinguishes the preconditions for the rise of 'rational capitalism', drawing to some extent upon Marx's analysis; on the other, he constructs an unhistorical 'ideal type' of this unique Western form of economy and society, in which the salient feature is precisely its rationality. This is not to say, however, that in Weber's account of Western society all historical movement is lacking. On the contrary, there is a clearly dominant tendency, but one which is not specifically 'capitalist' – the process of increasing 'rationalization' and 'mechanization' of life, which will probably, or even inevitably, continue whether the form of society is 'capitalist' or 'socialist'. It was, indeed, one of Weber's principal arguments against socialism that it would be more likely to lead to a 'dictatorship of the official' than to the 'dictatorship of the proletariat'; or, as he expressed this idea in his lecture on socialism (1918b):

> A progressive elimination of private capitalism is no doubt theoretically conceivable . . . . But assuming that it eventually happens, what would that mean in practice? The destruction of the iron cage of modern industrial labour? No! Rather that the administration of nationalized or 'socialized' enterprises too would become bureaucratic . . . . If private capitalism were eliminated the state bureaucracy would rule *alone*.

Weber's account of this dominant tendency in effect substitutes for a conception of 'capitalism' or 'socialism' that of 'industrial society': a form of society characterized by large-scale industrial production, technological rationality, the inexorable power of material goods, bureaucratic administration, and a pervasive 'calculating attitude'. In this respect Weber has been a major influence upon the later sociology of industrial (and post-industrial) societies, as is particularly evident in the writings of one of his most eminent followers, Raymond Aron[4]; although many of these more recent studies are far less critical in their orientation. For Weber, like Marx, though in different terms, saw the outcome of this process of industrialization and rationalization as the subordination of the human being to 'things', of the producer to the product (Löwith, 1932, pp. 48–9), and from this aspect there is also an affinity between his outlook and that of the Frankfurt School thinkers, in their emphasis upon technological rationality as a new form of domination (Bottomore, 1984b, pp. 36–8). Weber was not, for that matter, entirely enamoured of the specifically capitalist form of industrial society, and in his discussion of 'formal' and 'substantive' rationality (in *Economy and Society*, ch. 2, s. 9) he observes that while capitalism is rational in the sense of enhancing the calculability of economic action its rationality may well be problematic in terms of the ends which it promotes or the conditions of life which it imposes:

> The fact that the maximum of formal rationality in capital accounting is possible only provided that the workers are subjected to domination by the entrepreneurs is a further specific case of the substantive irrationality of the [capitalist] economic system.[5]

As I have suggested, there is lacking in Weber's account of this more or less ineluctable process of rationalization any conception of stages in the development of capitalism which might lead to its transformation into a radically different form of society, in particular as a result of its own internal tensions and conflicts. So far as Weber discerned any possibility of effective resistance to rationalization and the spread of bureaucratic regulation, which he portrayed as establishing a new 'house of serfdom', it was in the 'value-oriented' actions of individuals, especially in the shape of 'charismatic leaders'.[6] As Mommsen remarks (1974, pp. 102–3): 'Charisma emerges as the only creative revolutionary force in history, and, in a way, it is the only form in which the individual personality is capable of sensibly influencing the course of events in an age of ever more powerful bureaucracies.'

But even charisma does not offer any secure hope, for these individual creative interventions in history are themselves likely to be 'routinized' and absorbed in the remorseless development of capitalist (or equally, in Weber's view, socialist) industrialism.[7]

The other side of Weber's preoccupation with the creative actions of individuals – and especially those outstanding charismatic individuals – is his rejection of the idea of a 'revolutionary class', which occupies a central place in Marx's theory of history, and, more especially, of the development of capitalism. Weber, in his analysis of class, as in much of his other work, takes as his starting point Marx's theory of class; or, perhaps it would be truer to say, Marxist theory as it was currently expounded in Germany. In the chapter on 'classes, status groups and parties' in *Economy and Society* he initially defines classes in terms of 'property' and 'lack of property', which are 'the basic categories of all class situations', but he immediately qualifies this by observing that there is a further differentiation within these classes 'according to the kind of property that is usable for returns, and, on the other hand, according to the kind of services that can be offered in the market'. Hence, for Weber, classes 'are not communities; they merely represent possible, and frequent, bases for communal action'; and although, in his view, 'the factor that creates "class" is unambiguously economic interest . . . . nevertheless, the concept of "class interest" is an ambiguous one', and he concludes by saying that 'the rise of societal or even communal action from a common class situation is by no means a universal phenomenon'. Weber also observes that stratification by status interferes with the strict implementation of market principles, thus moderating class differences and antagonisms, and towards the end of his discussion he sketches the conditions in which 'class' or 'status' will be predominant:

> When the bases of the acquisition and distribution of goods are relatively stable, stratification by status is favoured. Every technological repercussion and economic transformation threatens stratification by status and pushes the class situation into the foreground. Epochs and countries in which the naked

class situation is of predominant significance are regularly the periods of technical and economic transformations.

Unlike Marx, however, Weber did not pursue his analysis of these 'economic transformations', and, although he recognized, in various contexts, the dominance exercised by the owners of property over those whose only resource is their labour power, the main tendency of his thought was to remove the concept of class from the sphere of production to that of the market (i.e. the sphere of exchange): ' "class situation" is, in this sense, ultimately "market situation" '. This amounts to dissolving the notion of 'class', and as Parkin (1982, p. 94) has concluded:

> Having in effect abandoned the distinction between capital and labour as the defining elements of class, Weber never proposes an alternative model. That is, he sets out no principles by which to locate the notional 'boundary' between a dominant or exploiting class and a subordinate or exploited class. What is portrayed instead is a Hobbesian war of all against all as each group fights its own corner in the anarchy of the market place.

For Weber, the principal tensions and struggles within capitalist society are those among individuals competing in the market, or among numerous, diverse groups aiming to promote their sectional interests; and notwithstanding some disagreeable consequences of this kind of struggle it has also to be seen as a fundamental element in capitalist dynamism and productivity, which creates the most favourable conditions for an 'open society'.[8] This emphasis upon the competitive struggle in which individuals and a plethora of interest groups are engaged is clearly intended to contest the idea of a polarization of social interests between 'two great classes', increasingly locked in conflict over the whole structure of society; and Weber's later writings (in *Economy and Society*, in his lecture on socialism, and in his commentaries on the postwar situation in Germany) are, like the works of his Marxist opponents, at the same time a political intervention, designed in his case to present a qualified defence of capitalism, and to diminish the significance of class struggles.

In another respect, however, Weber retained a very strong sense of the importance of class. At an early stage in his career (in his inaugural lecture at Freiburg in 1895) he declared a commitment to bourgeois values from which he never deviated; and, as Bahrdt (1971) has argued, his fundamental conviction was that 'the property-owning entrepreneurial bourgeoisie was the only group capable of providing the leadership to maintain a dynamic society'.[9] What is meant here by a 'dynamic society' is, however, something very different from the 'open society' which is presumed to result from individual competition in the market; namely, a society which is capable of engaging effectively in the competitive struggle among nation states for world power or pre-eminence. This aspect of Weber's thought, which has been quite indefensibly neglected by most later commentators,[10] is crucial in understanding his broader conception of class, for in his political writings, especially from 1918 onwards, Weber relates all political issues to the central question (from his standpoint) of reconstructing Germany as a powerful nation state, and consistently upholds the claim of a particular class – the bourgeoisie – to be the dominant power in society and its leading political force. In this context Weber's theoretical discussion of class as a basis for communal action takes on a more ambiguous character: the bourgeoisie now appears as a class which can indeed effectively dominate and lead society, and Weber's doubts about class 'interests' and class 'action' are seen to be directed primarily, if not solely, against the idea that the working class is capable of acting collectively to bring into existence a new form of society. It is the working class, not the bourgeoisie, which is 'dissolved' in Weber's thought. Similarly, whereas in *Economy and Society* Weber discusses in a rather inconclusive way the 'types of class struggle', and tends to reduce them, in the case of capitalist society, to 'market struggles' (e.g., over the price of labour), in his political writings the idea of class struggle emerges much more sharply in his sustained advocacy of bourgeois dominance, in opposition to the endeavours of the working-class movement, especially in its more radical forms, to gain power. This practical political orientation has to be seen in the context of the Russian Revolution, and of the intense class struggles in Germany from 1918 up to Weber's death.

The relation of Weber's conception of capitalism to Marx's theory is undoubtedly complex, but the principal affinities and divergences should now be apparent. In defining capitalism Weber recognizes the importance of those elements which Marx had emphasized; namely, private ownership of the means of production, the creation of a working class dependent for its existence and reproduction on the sale of its labour power, and the continuous transformation of the process of production through technology. As I have noted, it is in the *General Economic History* rather than in *The Protestant Ethic* that Weber is closest to Marx in his analysis of the preconditions for a capitalist economy; but even his thesis concerning the influence of Calvinism on the formation of a 'capitalist spirit' does not necessarily contradict Marx's account of the origins of capitalism, since it may well be regarded as drawing attention to an important additional factor in the explanation of that 'drive to accumulate' ('Accumulate, accumulate! That is Moses and the prophets' – *Capital*, Vol. 1, ch. 24) which Marx himself saw as the impelling force of bourgeois society.[11] Equally, Weber's emphasis upon rational law and administration, and the modern European nation state, as essential conditions for capitalist development is not incompatible with Marx's theory, in which 'political centralization', involving the creation of one nation, one code of laws, etc., is treated as a necessary concomitant of the bourgeoisie's rise to power (see especially the *Communist Manifesto*, s. 1). Here, as in the case of the 'capitalist spirit', the extent of the divergence between Marx and Weber has to be judged in terms of the degree of autonomy and causal significance assigned to the various elements;[12] and the circumstances which Weber identified as favourable to the rise of Western capitalism can be accommodated without difficulty, I think, in the framework of a Marxist theory which treats major historical changes as the outcome of interrelations and interactions among several elements in a total social structure.

The real distinctiveness of Weber's view of capitalism is to be found in the broad perspective which he adopts, and in what that perspective leads him to highlight or obscure. By contrast with

Marx, who puts in the foreground class domination in the sphere of production and class relations, Weber relates his analysis of capitalism to two quite different phenomena. The first is the process of rationalization, which Weber, as we have seen, presents as a dominant feature of the modern Western world, and one that is likely to persist in any conceivable future form of society. By this approach Weber succeeds in restricting the significance of the opposition between capitalism and socialism, and establishing the pre-eminence of an alternative conception of modern society as technological, industrial and bureaucratically regulated, with all its fateful consequences for the individual human being.

The second phenomenon (which is by no means brought into any clear relation with the first in Weber's thought) is the nation state, as a central point of reference for all economic and political studies. The 'absolute primacy of the interests of the nation state' is a basic, and unexamined, datum in Weber's social theory,[13] and his account of capitalism is profoundly influenced by it. Not only is the productive efficiency of capitalism vitally important for national power, but the bourgeoisie, despite all its shortcomings, is seen by Weber as the class most likely to provide effective national leadership. On the other hand, Weber's attitude to the revolutionary working-class movement in the postwar period was that its success would only weaken the German nation still further.

This discussion suggests that it was not capitalism as such (i.e. the development of the capitalist mode of production and the specific structure of a capitalist society) which constituted the central object of inquiry in Weber's social theory, but only certain aspects of it, which were related to his overriding concern, at one level, with 'rationalization' and, at another level, with the destiny of the German nation state. Such an assessment seems warranted, moreover, in view of the absence from Weber's work of any substantial, connected analysis of the structure of capitalist society, its place being taken, as he indicates in the prefatory note to Chapter 2 *Economy and Society*, by definitions of certain concepts and analyses of a number of sociological relationships in the economic sphere. How far these analyses, shaped by Weber's own preoccupations, are useful in explaining aspects of the subsequent course of capitalist development is a question to be taken up in a later chapter.

NOTES TO CHAPTER 2

1 Brubaker, 1984, ch. 1. The central importance of the concept of 'rationality' in social theory has been reaffirmed in the recent work of Habermas (1981), where a long chapter is devoted to examining in detail Weber's conception of the rationalization of modern society, and Habermas's own theory is presented as an analysis of the two principal forms of present-day rationalization: organized capitalism and bureaucratic socialism.

2 Weber, in the short introduction to his *Gesammelte Aufsätze zur Religionssoziologie* (1920), the English translation of which appears as the author's introduction to *The Protestant Ethic and the Spirit of Capitalism* (1976). See also the observation by Karl Löwith (1932) that for both Weber and Marx 'the sphere of their investigations is one and the same: the "capitalist" organization of a modern economy and society'.

3 This is, of course, the thesis expounded more fully in *The Protestant Ethic and the Spirit of Capitalism*, which has been the subject of much subsequent interpretation and debate. For excerpts from the critical literature see Green, 1959, and for a recent discussion of the main issues, Parkin, 1982, pp. 40–70.

4 See Aron, 1967a and 1967b.

5 See also the discussion in Brubaker, 1984, pp. 35–43.

6 In his conception of creative, 'value-oriented', individual action Weber was profoundly influenced by Nietzsche, as Mommsen (1974, pp. 103–7) and, even more strongly, Fleischmann (1964) have argued.

7 There is a close affinity between this aspect of Weber's thought and the ideas of the Frankfurt School, both in the emphasis upon individual values (especially by Horkheimer) and in the pessimistic conclusions about the assimilation and pacification of protest and rebellion (particularly in the later writings of Marcuse). See the discussion in Bottomore, 1984b, pp. 36–8, 41–3.

8 See the comments in this sense by Mommsen, 1974, p. 71.

9 Although as Löwith (1932, p. 106) observes, he was quite prepared to present 'some unpalatable truths to his own class' about its political failures.

10 It has been rescued from oblivion particularly by Mommsen (1959, 1974). See also my discussion in Bottomore, 1984a, ch. 7.

11 From this point of view the 'origins of capitalism' need to be analysed in terms of various structural conditions on one side, and of 'motivation' on the other, and whether the analysis is judged to be more 'Marxist' or more 'Weberian' will depend upon how the 'relative autonomy' of the different elements and the manner of their integration in a total social structure are conceived. For an interesting recent study, along these lines, of the absence of independent capitalist development in Scotland, see Marshall, 1980.

12 For example, in the case of the nation state, whether its emergence is conceived as a completely independent development or as being intimately connected with the rise of the bourgeoisie. Bauer (1907), for example, argues that 'every new economic order creates new forms of state

constitution and new rules for demarcating political structures', and Tilly (1975) observes that 'later on a powerful reciprocal relationship between the expansion of capitalism and the growth of state power developed'.

13 It may be noted here that, while Weber drew attention to the 'ambiguity' of the concept of 'class interest' and rejected the idea of classes as 'communities', he was inclined to take at face value 'national interests' and the 'national community', and certainly did not examine these concepts in the same critical manner.

3

Schumpeter's View of Capitalist Dynamism and Decline

Schumpeter's theory of capitalism has evident affinities on one side with Marx's ideas (and with some later Marxist views, notably those of the Austro-Marxists) and on the other side with those of Max Weber. Its distinctive feature, however, is Schumpeter's emphasis upon the role of the entrepreneur as the principal agent of capitalist development. In *The Theory of Economic Development* (1911, revised edition 1926) he conceives development or change as resulting from 'new combinations' of materials and forces in the sphere of production, a process which has three aspects. First, these new combinations 'are, as a rule, embodied . . . . in new firms which generally do not arise out of the old ones but start producing beside them', and he gives as an example that 'in general it is not the owner of stage coaches who builds railways'. (p. 66). Second, 'command over means of production is necessary to the carrying out of new combinations', and this is achieved above all by the use of credit, which Schumpeter sees as 'the characteristic method of the capitalist type of society . . . . for forcing the economic system into new channels'. (pp. 68–9). The third element is 'the fundamental phenomenon of economic development', namely, the entrepreneur or 'captain of industry'. Schumpeter summarizes his conception in the following terms

> . . . . the carrying out of new combinations is a special function, and the privilege of a type of people who are much less numerous than all those who have the 'objective'

possibility of doing it. Therefore, finally, entrepreneurs are a special type, and their behaviour a special problem, the motive power of a great number of significant phenomena. Hence our position may be characterised by three corresponding pairs of opposites. First, by the opposition of two real processes: the circular flow or the tendency towards equilibrium on the one hand, a change in the channels of economic routine or a spontaneous change in the economic data arising from within the system on the other. Secondly, by the opposition of two theoretical apparatuses: statics and dynamics. Thirdly, by the opposition of two types of conduct, which, following reality, we can picture as two types of individuals: mere managers and entrepreneurs. (pp. 81–3)

He then goes on to give a comprehensive description of the characteristic features of this 'special type' of individual, the captain of industry or business leader (pp. 83–94).[1] In a later work, *Business Cycles* (1939), Schumpeter summarized his view of capitalism as follows: 'Capitalism is that form of private property economy in which innovations are carried out by means of borrowed money, which in general, though not by logical necessity, implies credit creation' (Vol. 1, p. 223); and the individuals who carry out these innovations 'we call entrepreneurs'.

When Schumpeter turned subsequently to consider the later phases of capitalist development, and in particular the probable decline of capitalism (in *Capitalism, Socialism and Democracy*, 1942), the entrepreneur again had a central place in his analysis, but this time as an obsolescent 'type', for 'innovation itself is being reduced to a routine' (p. 132). The change in Schumpeter's thinking began in the 1920s, and its significance has been concisely formulated by Paul Sweezy:

> If I were asked to date the beginning of a distinctively bourgeois theory of the capitalist system as it has taken shape in the twentieth century, I think I would cite Schumpeter's article 'The Instability of Capitalism' which appeared in the *Economic Journal* (September 1928). There we not only find the giant corporation or trust as a characteristic feature of the system; even more important, this economic unit, so foreign

to the whole corpus of classical and neo-classical theory, provides the basis for new and important theoretical propositions. It will be recalled that in the Schumpeterian theory as set forth in *The Theory of Economic Development*, innovation is the function of the individual entrepreneur and that it is from the activity of innovating entrepreneurs that all the dynamic features of the system are directly or indirectly derived. These features include interest on money (absent from Schumpeter's 'circular flow'), the operations of the credit system, and the form of the business cycle. In 'The Instability of Capitalism', however, Schumpeter places the innovative function no longer in the individual entrepreneur but in the big corporation. At the same time innovation is reduced to a routine carried out by teams of specialists educated and trained for their jobs. In the Schumpeterian scheme of things, these are absolutely basic changes destined to produce equally basic changes in capitalism's *modus operandi*'. (1972, pp. 31–2)

In *Capitalism, Socialism and Democracy*, Schumpeter analysed these changes much more fully, from a broad sociological perspective, and expounded more systematically a general view of the tendency of capitalism to 'destroy itself' and to create the conditions for the emergence of 'centralist socialism'. Since I have discussed Schumpeter's principal arguments in some detail elsewhere,[2] I will summarize them quite briefly here, noting particularly their affinities with some of the arguments of Max Weber, and of Marx and later Marxists. There are, according to Schumpeter, three main factors which account for the prospective decline of capitalism. The first, referred to by Sweezy in the passage just cited, is what Schumpeter called the 'obsolescence of the entrepreneurial function', which results partly from the growth of large corporations, partly from the creation, by capitalism, of an environment in which economic change is accepted as a matter of course, and there is less resistance needing to be overcome by entrepreneurial energy and will power; in Schumpeter's words, 'economic progress tends to become depersonalized and automatized. Bureau and committee work tends to replace individual action' (p. 133). This decline

of the entrepreneur also has wider consequences, for it 'affects
the position of the entire bourgeois stratum . . . . The perfectly
bureaucratized giant industrial unit not only ousts the small or
medium-sized firm and "expropriates" its owners, but in the end
it also ousts the entrepreneur and expropriates the bourgeoisie as
a class' (p. 134). Hence the bourgeoisie – deprived of its vital
element, the entrepreneur – increasingly loses the will and the
capacity to defend capitalism.

The second major factor undermining the political defences of
capitalism is the gradual 'destruction of the protecting strata'
and of the institutional framework. In Schumpeter's view the
bourgeoisie is an unheroic, or (to make use of Weber's term)
a 'non-charismatic', class; the industrialist and merchant has
'surely no trace of any mystic glamour about him which is what
counts in the ruling of men. The stock exchange is a poor
substitute for the Holy Grail' (p. 137). Where the bourgeois
strata did attempt to rule directly 'they did not make a
conspicuous success of ruling', and they fared better, according
to Schumpeter, when (as in England) they allowed the feudal,
aristocratic element to rule on their behalf (pp. 136–7). But as
capitalism continues to develop the pre-capitalist social
framework is broken down, and the 'protecting master' is
eliminated, thus removing one of the buttresses that prevented a
political collapse. At the same time, other sources of support for
capitalism are eroded as industrial concentration eliminates large
numbers of small producers and traders (here, says Schumpeter,
'Marx scores'). Furthermore, with the growth of large corporations in which the leading elements are the salaried executives
and managers, together with the large and small shareholders,
'the figure of the proprietor and with it the specifically
proprietary interest have vanished . . . . Thus the capitalist
process pushes into the background all those institutions, the
institutions of property and free contracting in particular, that
expressed the needs and ways of the truly "private" economic
activity' (pp. 141–2).

Finally, capitalism engenders a rational and critical frame of
mind which can be turned against it, and 'the bourgeois finds to
his amazement that the rationalist attitude does not stop at the
credentials of Kings and popes but goes on to attack private

property and the whole scheme of bourgeois values'.[3] What is more, it produces ('by the very logic of its civilization') a social group – the intellectuals – which has 'a vested interest in social unrest'. Capitalism let the intellectual loose and 'presented him with the printing press' (pp. 146–7), and it is the modern intellectuals who stimulate, verbalize and organize the materials of social discontent, notably through their relations with the labour movement.

In Schumpeter's theory, as I have said, there are many filiations with the ideas of Weber and Marx. Like Weber, Schumpeter associates capitalist development with a process of rationalization, and while he rejects the notion that the rational 'calculating attitude' is specifically modern (see note 1 to this chapter), regarding it as a prevalent feature in all forms of human society (forced upon the human mind, in his view, by economic necessity), he goes on to argue that:

> Capitalism develops rationality and adds a new edge to it in two interconnected ways. First it exalts the monetary unit – not itself a creation of capitalism – into a unit of account. That is to say, capitalist practice turns the unit of money into a tool of rational cost-profit calculations, of which the towering monument is double-entry bookkeeping[4] .... And thus defined and quantified for the economic sector, this type of logic or attitude or method then starts upon its conqueror's career, subjugating – rationalizing – man's tools and philosophies, his medical practice, his picture of the cosmos, his outlook on life, everything in fact including his concepts of beauty and justice and his spiritual aspirations .... Second, rising capitalism produced not only the mental attitude of modern science .... but also the men and the means .... by creating the social space for a new class that stood upon individual achievement in the economic field, it in turn attracted to that field the strong wills and the strong intellects.
> (*Capitalism, Socialism and Democracy*, pp. 123–4)

Schumpeter differs profoundly from Weber, however, in his view of the consequences of rationalization, which he conceives as producing not a 'mechanized petrifaction' but the decline of capitalism and the probable advent of a socialist economy. This happens for two reasons, which I indicated earlier: one is that the functions of innovation and entrepreneurship are increasingly taken over by a rationalized, bureacratic form of management; the other, that the rational, critical attitude comes to be directed against the capitalist social order itself, 'against private property and the whole scheme of bourgeois values' (p. 143). In discussing the first of these processes he again diverges from Weber in his evaluation of bureaucracy; and indeed he directly attacks Weber's position (among others) when he raises 'the question of that Bureaucratization of Economic Life which constitutes the theme of so many anti-socialist homilies':

> I for one cannot visualize, in the condition of modern society, a socialist organization in any form other than that of a huge and all-embracing bureaucratic apparatus. Every other possibility I can conceive would spell failure and breakdown. But surely this should not horrify anyone who realizes how far the bureaucratization of economic life – of life in general even – has gone already and who knows how to cut through the underbrush of phrases that has grown up around the subject. (p. 206)

Schumpeter then goes on to examine, in a spirit very different from that of Weber, the relation of bureaucracy to democracy, observing that it is 'not an obstacle to democracy but an inevitable complement to it', just as it is 'an inevitable complement to modern economic development' (ibid.):

> . . . . democratic government in modern industrial society must be able to command . . . . the services of a well-trained bureaucracy of good standing and tradition, endowed with a strong sense of duty and a no less strong *esprit de corps* . . . . It must also be strong enough to guide and, if need be, to instruct the politicians who head the ministries. In order to be able to do this it must be in a position to evolve principles of its own and sufficiently independent to assert them. It must be a power in its own right . . . . The bureaucracies of Europe . . . . exemplify very well what I am trying to convey. They are

the product of a long development that started with the *ministeriales* of medieval magnates . . . . and went on through the centuries until the powerful engine emerged which we behold today. It cannot be created in a hurry . . . . But it grows everywhere, whatever the political method a nation may adopt. Its expansion is the one certain thing about our future. (pp. 293–4)

This passage does not only convey Schumpeter's very positive evaluation of the role of bureaucracy (i.e. rational administration) in modern society. It also reaffirms an important theme in his whole conception of capitalism, mentioned earlier in relation to the 'protecting strata' – namely, that the successful development of a capitalist economy has depended heavily upon the persistence of a social framework constituted by pre-capitalist institutions and cultural norms. Schumpeter, it may be claimed, emphasizes more strongly than do Marx and Weber the element of continuity in social systems,[5] and this view is formulated in more general terms in his essay on social classes (1927):

Every social situation is the heritage of preceding situations and takes over from them not only their cultures, their dispositions, and their 'spirit', but also elements of their social structure and concentrations of power . . . . This means that in explaining any historical course or situation, account must be taken of the fact that much in it can be explained only by the survival of elements that are actually alien to its own trends. (pp. 144–5)

Nevertheless, there *are* social transformations and the emergence of new social 'types', however much baggage from the past they may carry with them, and Schumpeter's emphasis upon the role of the entrepreneur, as a new and special 'type', in the development of capitalism shows a further affinity with Weber's analysis. In the *General Economic History* Weber defined capitalism broadly as a system of production carried on 'by the method of enterprise', and as I indicated in the previous chapter he went on to relate his argument concerning the influence of the Protestant ethic directly to the role of the entrepreneur via the concept of a 'calling', which gave the modern entrepreneur 'a fabulously clear conscience', and 'industrious workers'. In *The Protestant Ethic*, drawing upon Sombart's study *Der moderne Kapitalismus*, Weber discusses at greater length the role of the entrepreneur and makes a distinction between the 'traditional' and the 'innovating' entrepreneur, the latter being a product of the 'spirit of capitalism', itself largely shaped, according to Weber's thesis, by the Protestant ethic.

If we now compare these accounts of the entrepreneur by Weber and Schumpeter, the major differences appear to be that, on one side, Schumpeter undertakes a much more thorough economic analysis of the functions of the entrepreneur, while on the other side he deliberately leaves aside the problem of the historical origins of the innovating entrepreneur, saying that 'no historical evolutionary factors will be indicated . . . . like changes in the mentality of economic men . . . . and so forth' (*Theory of Economic Development*, pp. 60–1). It is an interesting question whether Weber's and Schumpeter's studies of the entrepreneur could be assimilated, partially at least, into Marx's theory. I suggested in the previous chapter that the Protestant ethic thesis might be seen as providing a supplementary explanation of the urge to accumulate, and Schumpeter's conception of the innovating entrepreneur could perhaps be treated in a similar way. But it is clear that Marx attributes much greater importance to structural factors, and in particular that he conceives accumulation, once capitalist production is established, as being the consequence, in the context of technological progress, of competition among individual capitalists, who are thereby compelled to save and invest, whatever their particular psychological dispositions. Moreover, in so far as Weber and Schumpeter use the concept of the entrepreneur in a theory of profit, treated as the reward for innovation and risk-taking, their analysis is wholly incompatible with Marx's theory. There is, however, again some convergence of ideas in Schumpeter's view of a later stage of capitalist development in which the entrepreneurial function declines in importance (and perhaps also, in a less rigorously argued form, in Weber's characterization of a developed capitalist society as one in which, whereas 'the Puritan wanted to have a calling, we are obliged to have one'); for here the structural, institutional factors become pre-eminent, and Schumpeter, as we have seen, attributes a major influence to the growth of large corporations, which Marx discussed in terms of the centralization and concentration of capital, and the emergence of the joint-stock company.

Schumpeter's work is, without question, closely related to, and much influenced by, Marxist theory. Unlike Weber, Schumpeter had a profound knowledge not only of Marx's own writings but also of the works of the most significant later Marxist thinkers, particularly in the economic field;[6] and the first part of *Capitalism, Socialism and Democracy* is devoted to an illuminating exposition of the basic elements of the theory, lavishing praise upon Marx's achievements as economist and sociologist while being highly critical of many of his detailed arguments. Schumpeter agrees with Marx, so far as the theory of capitalism is concerned,[7] in several important respects (see especially Chapter 3 of *Capitalism, Socialism and Democracy*). First, he emphasizes the value of Marx's view of capitalism as a dynamic process, in which 'economic progress . . . . means turmoil', and notes that 'Marx saw this process of industrial change more clearly and he realized its pivotal importance more fully than any other economist of his time'. Second, he argues that Marx's theory of concentration, in spite of some inadequacies, correctly predicted the advent of big business and perceived some of its consequences. Third, although Marx 'had no simple theory of business cycles', and in Schumpeter's view could not derive one strictly from the 'laws' of the capitalist process, nevertheless there is to be found in Marx's work 'practically all the elements that ever entered into any serious analysis of the business cycle, and on the whole very little error'. Finally, while disputing some of Marx's 'facts and reasoning', Schumpeter agrees with his conclusion that 'capitalist evolution will destroy the foundations of capitalist society'. According to Schumpeter's own argument, as he develops it with various qualifications in *Capitalism, Socialism and Democracy*, the economic process tends to socialize itself, and it is capitalism which 'shapes things and souls for socialism' (p. 220). The argument is very close, in many respects, to the views of the Austro-Marxists, especially Renner

(1916) in his discussion of the economic consequences of the First World War, and above all Hilferding (1915, 1924a, 1927) in his elaboration of the notion of 'organized capitalism' as a phase of transition to socialism.

Where Schumpeter's theory diverges most radically from Marxism is in its rejection of the idea of class struggle as a major factor in the development, and eventual decline, of capitalism. In the first part of *Capitalism, Socialism and Democracy* Schumpeter insists upon the great diversity to be found in the definitions of class, and in the interpretations of class interest and class action; the whole subject, he claims, 'is a hotbed of prejudices to this day, and as yet hardly in its scientific stage' (p. 14). From this point he goes on to argue that Marx's 'exaggeration of the definiteness and importance of the dividing line between the capitalist class . . . . and the proletariat was surpassed only by the exaggeration of the antagonism between them', and further (in an astonishing assertion) that 'socialism . . . . in reality has nothing to do with the presence or absence of social classes'. Not surprisingly, therefore, classes and class struggles have no place in the argument of the rest of the book, where Schumpeter also goes to extreme lengths to exclude any socialist definition of socialism (above all, in terms of 'classlessness') and to restrict the meaning of the word to the narrowly economic, and sociologically indeterminate, sense of 'an institutional pattern in which the control over means of production and over production is vested with a central authority' (p. 167).

In this crucial part of his theory Schumpeter stands much closer to Weber than to Marx, while taking an even more extreme view than does Weber of the relative unimportance of classes in explaining capitalist development. It is on this point, particularly, that it will be necessary, in a later chapter, to compare the theories of Marx, Weber and Schumpeter with respect to their usefulness in understanding the nature, and the probable course of development, of capitalist societies in the late twentieth century.

NOTES TO CHAPTER 3

1 It should be remarked here that Schumpeter distinguishes his own view from that of Max Weber by emphasizing the prevalence of a 'calculating attitude' in non-capitalist economies, and arguing that 'the choice of new methods is not simply an element in the concept of rational economic action, nor a matter of course, but a distinct process which stands in need of special explanation' (p. 80, footnote).

2 See Tom Bottomore, Introduction to the 5th edition of *Capitalism, Socialism and Democracy* (1976); and Tom Bottomore, 'The decline of capitalism', in Heertje, 1981, reprinted in Bottomore, 1984a.

3 In his article of 1928, 'The instability of capitalism', Schumpeter mentioned not only the growth of the large corporation and the decline of the entrepreneur, but also the spread of 'rationality', as an element of weakness in the capitalist system: 'Capitalism, whilst economically stable, and even gaining in stability, creates, by rationalizing the human mind, a mentality and style of life incompatible with its own fundamental conditions, motives and social institutions, and will be changed, although not by economic necessity and probably even at some sacrifice of economic welfare, into an order of things which will be merely a matter of taste and terminology to call Socialism or not'. It is evident that the germ of Schumpeter's later analysis was already present in this article.

4 Schumpeter notes that this element was particularly stressed by Sombart, but it also had a prominent place in Weber's analysis, in the *General Economic History* (especially chs. 17 and 22).

5 See the discussion of this feature of Schumpeter's thought, in relation to capitalism and imperialism, by Kumar, in Ellis and Kumar, 1983, pp. 157–62.

6 Knowledge which was transmitted in part through the Austro-Marxist thinkers, with whom Schumpeter was acquainted in his student days (see Smithies, 1951, p. 11).

7 He also had a high regard for the more general features of Marx's theoretical scheme; thus he observes that 'the so-called Economic Interpretation of History is doubtless one of the greatest individual achievements of sociology to this day', and that its two main propositions – namely, (i) 'the forms or conditions of production are the fundamental determinants of social structures which in turn breed attitudes, actions and civilizations', and (ii) 'the forms of production themselves have a logic of their own . . . . undoubtedly contain a large amount of truth and are . . . . invaluable working hypotheses' (*Capitalism, Socialism and Democracy*, pp. 10–12).

4

Capitalism, Individualism and Freedom

In the theories I have discussed so far an analysis of the structure and development of capitalism is interwoven with judgements on its merits and defects, especially in relation to the socialist movement. The distinctive feature of the theory now to be examined is that it does not put forward any systematic analysis of capitalist society, but is elaborated as a political philosophy concerned with the defence of individual liberty. The most eminent exponent of this doctrine, F. A. Hayek, declares indeed that:

> we use this term [capitalism] here because it is the most familiar name, but only with great reluctance, since with its modern connotations it is itself largely a creation of that socialist interpretation of economic history with which we are concerned. The term is especially misleading when, as is often the case, it is connected with the idea of the rise of a propertyless proletariat, which by some devious process have been deprived of the rightful ownership of the tools for their work. (1954, p. 15)

Later in the same text, therefore, Hayek refers to this form of society as 'industrial society', a usage which became widespread in the 1950s and 1960s among social scientists who held that the opposition between capitalism and socialism is now in some way *dépassé*, in the era of 'managed capitalism' and the 'mixed economy'.[1]

This is not, of course, Hayek's own view, and in his recent major exposition of his ideas, *Law, Legislation and Liberty* (1982), he has adopted as a description of Western capitalist society the term 'Great Society', which he claims to derive from Adam Smith[2] and to use in the same sense as Popper's 'open society'.[3] The Great Society is a 'self-generating or spontaneous order' (p. 2), and he cites approvingly Adam Smith's notion of the 'invisible hand' by which an individual intent only upon his own gain is led 'to promote an end which was no part of his intention', while decrying Smith's critics who 'cannot conceive of an order which is not deliberately made', but only of one 'aiming at concrete purposes which is . . . . what a spontaneous order cannot do' (pp. 37–8). But he does not notice Smith's further comment 'Nor is it *always* the worse for the society that it was no part of it' (my italics), which suggests, in a manner congruent with Smith's moral philosophy, that some kind of balance is needed between private interests and the public good (see note 2). Hayek's underlying conception of a spontaneous order also diverges widely from the ideas expressed by Popper, who speaks approvingly of the 'conscious alteration' of social institutions, or in other words of the desirability of a 'constructed society' such as Hayek abjures. In general, Popper's arguments concerning the 'open society' seem to have their source in a style of thought – 'constructivist rationalism' – which Hayek particularly condemns (pp. 24–34).

There is no reason, therefore, to connect Hayek's theory especially closely with conceptions of the 'open society' or the 'great society'. What the latter term means in his thought is simply a free-market economy, or *laissez-faire* capitalism,[4] which is contrasted with totalitarian 'socialist' or 'planned' economy. In this respect Hayek's view resembles to some extent that of Max Weber, but it takes a much more extreme form. Weber, it is true, thought that a planned economy would diminish individual freedom by increasing the degree of bureaucratic regulation, but at the same time he took as a central theme the processes of rationalization and mechanization that were already characteristic of capitalist societies and perhaps inescapable in any modern industrial society. For Weber, the problem of creating or maintaining a sphere of freedom for the individual has a complexity which Hayek ignores, and rational discussion of it requires not only a philosophical analysis but painstaking study of the actual development of the mode of production and social institutions in an industrial society, whether its form is capitalist or socialist.

What Hayek singles out for attention in his defence of capitalism is on one side its economic success, and on the other the connection which he claims to establish between a free-enterprise economy and individual freedom. His standpoint on the first of these themes is most sharply expressed in an essay (1954) introducing a collection of studies intended to reassess the effects of capitalism on the working class, in opposition to the 'socialist interpretation of history', where he argues that capitalism brought about an 'enormous improvement of their position'. But his view of the success of capitalism is presented mainly in negative terms, in studies of the problems of a planned economy (Hayek, 1949), and it is nowhere developed as fully as by Schumpeter (1942), or by Marx, in many of his works, where the significance of capitalism as a highly progressive stage in the development of human society is constantly emphasized.

There is also absent from Hayek's discussion any consideration of the historical development of capitalism (and hence of its transformations and the possible limits to its expansion), or on the other hand, of its contradictory features and internal tensions, and those less agreeable concomitants of its economic success which Weber, as well as Marx, observed. On the first matter Hayek's thought contrasts sharply with that of Schumpeter. The latter, as we have seen, treats the recent stage of capitalist development as one in which the entrepreneur is 'vanishing' and his function is being taken over by the large corporation, or increasingly by the state. This is a 'march into socialism', which Schumpeter regards as being quite compatible with continued economic progress. Hayek, on the other hand, pays scant attention to the growth of large corporations,[5] emphasizes the continuing importance of the entrepreneur and competitive markets, and directs his principal, sustained criticism against the economically harmful activities of the interventionist state. If, however, we look at the actual economic development of Western capitalism since 1945 (that is, during a period of massive and increasing state intervention in the economy), it emerges that the annual average rate of growth of the gross domestic product (GDP) and GDP per capita between

1950 and 1973 was more than twice as high as at any time between 1820 and 1950.[6] Or to take a specific recent example: Britain, which has had since 1979 a government committed to a Hayekian view of capitalism, is now characterized by social decay, increasing public squalor, massive unemployment, and economic decline, while Hayek's homeland, Austria, where the Socialist Party has had a profound influence on economic policy and was the governing party from 1971 until recently, is a prosperous country with low unemployment and a much higher rate of economic growth.

In terms of material living standards, therefore, it appears that the most successful phase of capitalist development has been the era of 'managed capitalism'; but whether this is to be regarded as a stage in some inescapable process of socialization of the economy, and a halfway house on the road to socialism, as Schumpeter argued, is a question to be examined later. Hayek's advocacy of *laissez-faire* capitalism and minimal government is not, in any case, based primarily upon arguments concerning economic efficiency, but upon the claim that there is a close and necessary relation between an unhampered free-market economy and individual freedom, conceived as the supreme good. This general proposition is upheld by a variety of arguments throughout Hayek's writings,[7] and in order to assess it we need first to distinguish carefully between its different elements.

One important starting point for Hayek's view of the emergence of the Great Society, and of what he calls 'liberalism' or 'individualism', is the contrast which he draws between early capitalism and the kind of economy and society that preceded it in western Europe, with respect to the freedom of individual action (above all, economic activity) which it allowed. This is expounded in very abstract terms, without any reference to historical studies, but it seems to conform quite closely with the accounts given by historians of the rise of capitalism from the fifteenth century,[8] and to express a commonly accepted view that the dissolution of feudal social relations through the growth of towns and the development of commerce and handicrafts did create a new space for individual activity and enlarge the sphere of human freedom – a change that was partially summed up in the phrase 'Town air makes free'.[9] Marx took a similar view, though with various qualifications, in arguing that early forms of society were founded upon an 'immature development of human beings as individuals' and that bourgeois society, for the first time, made apparent the distinction between the 'personal' and the 'class' individual, the 'accidental conditions of life for the individual', and revealed the possibilities for a full development of individuality while still restricting it through class domination.

Hayek concentrates, however, in his discussion of individualism and liberty, upon the nineteenth century, and here his interpretation is far more controversial. This period, in which industrial capitalism became established as the dominant mode of production in western Europe and North America, was characterized not only by increasing freedom of economic activity, represented by the emergence on one side of the entrepreneur, and on the other, of 'free' labour – a situation which Marx described in less glowing terms as one where all previous social bonds had been destroyed, leaving 'no other nexus between man and man than naked self-interest, than callous "cash payment" ' – but also by the development of the labour movement as a defence against, and then opposition to, capitalist society. It was this labour movement which – from its beginnings in political clubs, attempts at trade union organization, and co-operative ventures, through Chartism and the revolutions of 1848, to the socialist parties and mass trade unions of the late nineteenth century and the twentieth century – greatly extended individual liberty by its struggles for universal suffrage, for the right to form associations, for the control of economic power and the implementation of extensive social reforms, aided by those liberals turned radicals whose ideas and influence Hayek ignores.

Hence socialism always appeared as a liberating movement within capitalism and did indeed liberate millions of people by giving them greater control over their conditions of life, both at work and as consumers (for example, of housing, health services and education). It is only in the last half-century, and more particularly since the Second World War, that another image of socialism has emerged, in which it appears as an 'authoritarian' or 'totalitarian' form of society. This image, derived from the reality of Stalinism in Eastern Europe, forms the background to Hayek's defence of capitalism. His argument, that is to say, is largely negative in character, not exploring the actual extent of liberty in all the various contexts of life in Western capitalist society, but contrasting an abstractly conceived liberty and individuality with the lack of freedom in Soviet-type societies. The argument runs through all Hayek's work, from *The Road to Serfdom* (1944) to *Law, Legislation and Liberty* (1982), but it is extended far beyond the Soviet example to assert that *any* form of socialism 'would mean the destruction of freedom . . . . democratic socialism, the great utopia of the last few generations, is not only unachievable, but . . . . to strive for it produces something so utterly different that few of those who now wish it would be prepared to accept the consequences' (1944, p. 23), and later that 'socialism as much as fascism or communism inevitably leads into the totalitarian state and the destruction of the democratic order' (1982, Vol. 3, p. 151). Against this threat the only defence is to maintain 'that self-forming order of the market which serves the general good', which socialism would replace with 'a forcibly imposed order determined by some arbitrary human will' (ibid.)

It lies beyond the scope of this book to examine Hayek's conception of socialism[10] or the peculiar ethical theory which buttresses his notion of a spontaneous order.[11] The question to be considered here is whether his work contributes anything significant to a theory of capitalism, and the answer must be: very little. What he provides is advocacy, not analysis, conspicuous chiefly for its total lack of concern with the structure of a capitalist society, including its class structure, with the historical development of capitalism, and with any empirical considerations about the nature and extent of the diverse kinds of liberty and individualism to be found in modern societies.[12] In this sense Hayek's work is in no way comparable with the studies by Marx, Weber, and Schumpeter, and its principal contribution to the theory of capitalism is, so to speak an 'unintended consequence' of what is expressed in it – namely, a revelation of the ideology of capitalism in the late twentieth century. From this point of view it will need to be reconsidered in a later chapter.

NOTES TO CHAPTER 4

1 See especially Aron (1967a), who observes that 'I think we can say that the idea of industrial society is likely to be prominent at times when economists and politicians are inclined to emphasize the *forces of production*, science and technology, and to play down the importance of the economic system, whether this is defined by the property system or by the method of economic regulation (by the market or by planning)' (p. 3).

2 But this misrepresents what Adam Smith actually says in *The Wealth of Nations* (Book 5, ch. 1), where he contrasts the situation of 'a man of rank and fortune' who is 'by his rank and station the distinguished member of a great society, who attend to every part of his conduct, and who therefore oblige him to attend to every part of it himself', with that of 'a man of low condition', who is 'far from being a member of any great society' and 'as soon as he comes into a great city he is sunk in obscurity and darkness. His conduct is observed and attended to by nobody, and he is therefore very likely to neglect it himself, and to abandon himself to every sort of low profligacy and vice.' For Adam Smith, as is evident from his *Theory of Moral Sentiments*, the 'great society' is not simply a spontaneous order created by the pursuit of self-interest, but one which is regulated by custom, morality and education; that is, by general conceptions of what constitutes a decent or good society.

3 Popper (1945) certainly contrasts the 'open society', 'in which individuals are confronted with personal decisions', with a collectivist society as well as with tribal society (as forms of 'closed society'), but in enlarging upon his view he says that 'the transition [from the closed society to the open] takes place when social institutions are first consciously recognized as man-made, and when their conscious alteration is discussed in terms of their suitability for the achievement of human aims and purposes. Or, putting the matter in a less abstract way, the closed society breaks down when the supernatural awe with which the social order is considered gives way to active interference, and to the conscious pursuit of personal or group interests' (Vol. 1, p. 247). This seems to diverge substantially from Hayek's notion of a 'spontaneous order'.

4 After a somewhat vague discussion of the rules of conduct necessary to produce or sustain a spontaneous order, he refers in a specific way only to one form of society, which undoubtedly serves as his general model, namely 'a modern society based on exchange', in which 'one of the chief regularities in individual behaviour will result from the similarity of situations in which most individuals find themselves in working to earn an income', although he adds that 'people must also obey some conventional rules' if the resulting order is to be 'beneficial' (p. 45).

5 Only a few pages of *Law, Legislation and Liberty* (mainly in Vol. 3, pp. 77–80) are devoted to a very superficial discussion of them.

6 See Angus Maddison, 1982, Table 4.9 on p. 91, and the accompanying discussion.

7 It has also been formulated, of course, in many less sophisticated, more popular works (e.g., Milton Friedmann, 1962), and in its most simplistic form it has become a slogan of right-wing political leaders who identify the 'free world' (which includes a considerable number of savage military dictatorships) with a 'free-enterprise' economy.

8 See especially Fernand Braudel, 1981–4.

9 But a recent historian, Alan Macfarlane, has argued (1978) that England was

a special case, in that a considerable degree of individual freedom and mobility existed already in the thirteenth century, on the basis of widespread private ownership of land, and that this distinctiveness may explain why the industrial revolution emerged first there (pp. 189–203).

10   His arguments concerning socialist planning and calculation will be discussed in a forthcoming work, Tom Bottomore, *The Socialist Economy in Theory and Practice.*

11   Hayek appears to adopt the standpoint of Max Weber, that there are conflicts between different 'value-orientations' which cannot be resolved by reason (see Brubaker, 1984). Thus he argues (1982, Vol. 2, p. 15) that the Great Society is pluralistic in the sense that 'it is governed by a multiplicity of individual ends' which cannot be brought into harmony in some rational order of social purposes (for instance, in a generally agreed conception of social justice), but at the same time he claims that it is possible to have agreement on the 'rules of just conduct' (apparently either as the outcome of rational discussion, in the case of legislation, or by following some unexamined 'tradition') and that 'the social world is governed in the long run by certain moral principles on which the people at large believe' (1982, Vol. 3, p. 151). This is a medley of confused argument, complemented by misrepresentation of his opponents' views – e.g., that 'egalitarianism preaches that nobody is better that anybody else' (ibid., p. 172). In what text? Certainly not in one of the most widely read expositions, by Tawney (1952), or in my own writing on the subject, where I explicitly reject this idea as 'foolish' (Bottomore 1964, p. 129).

12   See the comments by Lukes (1973), in his general study of individualism, on 'the ever-growing gap between the economic individualist model and the corporate neo-capitalist reality', and on Hayek's 'extremely narrow and tendentious definition of liberty, which would preclude calling violations of liberty most of the characteristic evils of capitalism' (pp. 153–4).

5

Imperialism and the Stages of Capitalist Development

Marx, Weber, and Schumpeter all conceived capitalism as a dynamic form of society which manifests definite tendencies of development; and they made predictions about its future, at least in Schumpeter's 'weak' sense of trying to 'diagnose observable tendencies and to state what results would be, if these tendencies should work themselves out according to their logic', while taking into account 'resistances' or counter-tendencies which might arrest the development at 'some halfway house' (1942, p. 422). With the benefit of hindsight we can now reassess their views against the background of a century of capitalist development in a rapidly changing world situation, and attempt a new analysis of the main tendencies and counter-tendencies. In doing so, however, we must recognize the substantial differences between the three thinkers. Not only did they write from different social and historical vantage points, which profoundly affected their judgement of events, but the subsequent development, or lack of development, of their ideas followed very different paths. Marx's theory gave rise to a school – or, more precisely, diverse and often divergent schools – of thought within which it has been continuously revised and reformulated. Weber's analysis, by contrast, was not extensively discussed.[1] The main debate has revolved almost entirely around his thesis concerning the *origins* of Western capitalism,[2] and only in recent years, as will be seen, has greater attention been given to the theme of rationalization as a central feature of capitalist development. Similarly, Schumpeter's later work, *Capitalism,*

Socialism and Democracy, though widely read, did not generate the kind of theoretical debate which might have been expected, and his ideas have only recently been critically reassessed (Heertje, 1981), but again without giving rise, apparently, to any extensive discussion.

The first major reconsideration of Marx's theory occurred at the end of the nineteenth century in the so-called 'revisionist' controversy animated by Bernstein (1899), who argued that the theory required modification to take account of recent changes in Western capitalism – changes which he summarized in the following way: 'Peasants do not sink; middle class does not disappear; crises do not grow ever larger; misery and serfdom do not increase.'[3] In one form or another these themes, and especially the last three, have remained at the centre of the controversies within (and around) Marxist social theory. Above all, Bernstein emphasized the significance of the changes in class structure and in the conditions of life of the working class: property ownership was becoming more widespread, the general level of living was rising, the middle class was increasing rather than declining in numbers, the structure of capitalist society was not being simplified but was becoming more complex and differentiated, and in consequence there was not a growing polarization of classes. The mature phase of capitalism, it might be claimed from this standpoint, was coming to resemble those earlier epochs of history described in the *Communist Manifesto*, when there was 'almost everywhere a complicated arrangement of society into various orders, a manifold gradation of social rank'. In this sense, too, it might be argued – as has been done frequently in later studies[4] – that Marx's theory of classes can usefully be complemented by Weber's analysis of the social and political significance of status groups in capitalist society.

Ever since Bernstein published his 'revisionist' thesis, Marxist sociologists, and their critics, have returned again and again to the problems of class structure and of the political role of classes in the development of capitalism. The outcome, or present state, of this long-continued discussion is far from clear,[5] at any rate in the sense of having attained some definite and broadly accepted view, either among Marxists or between Marxists and their opponents. One notable common feature of all these studies, however, is their profoundly unhistorical (and, in a wider sense, insufficiently sociological) approach. Some twenty years ago, at the end of a book on social classes (Bottomore, 1965), I distinguished as the principal fault of many recent studies their lack of a historical sense, and concluded that a comprehensive historical analysis of the changing class structure in modern societies remained one of the most important unfulfilled tasks of sociology. It is still largely unfulfilled today. Over the past two decades studies of class, and in particular Marxist studies, have either been devoted mainly to conceptual analysis (e.g., Poulantzas, 1973, 1975; Carchedi, 1977; Wright, 1978) or, where they deal with empirical matters, have been concerned with relatively short time spans and/or with the situation of a particular class (often in a single country), without locating it clearly in the general structure of class relations (e.g., Braverman, 1974; Abercrombie and Urry, 1983). These empirical studies can be seen as forming part of a long series, beginning with Bernstein's work and continuing through Lederer's (1912) study of salaried employees, Max Adler's (1933) analysis of the 'metamorphosis of the working class', and Renner's (1953) discussion of the 'service class', to the debates of the 1950s about the 'affluent worker' and those of the present time about the decline of class alignment in voting behaviour.

The recurrence of the same questions over a period of almost a century now[6] indicates that Marx's theory of the conflict between two major classes, as a fundamental element in the development of capitalism, is far from having been superseded. On a long historical view several different aspects of this development need to be distinguished: the changing situation and degree of organization of various classes, the changes in the economic and political conditions of their struggles, the contradictory elements which emerge in the course of development through the formation of tendencies and counter-tendencies, and the related fluctuations in political orientation and action. Thus on one side the position of different classes has unmistakably changed, whether we consider the occupational structure or the main spheres of economic activity. The proportion of manual workers in the labour force has declined from some 80 per cent at the beginning of the twentieth century to around 50 per cent in the 1980s, while the proportion of professional and clerical workers has correspondingly increased.[7] This is clearly related to changes in the sectoral pattern of production and employment: agricultural employment has declined steadily (and more rapidly since 1950), while industrial employment rose to a peak of just below 50 per cent of the employed population and then began to decline, and employment in services has continued to increase until it now represents well over half of total employment.[8] Over the same period, as a consequence of the increasing productivity of labour, per capita income rose substantially, notably between 1950 and the early 1970s, thus engendering the debate about the 'affluent worker'.

But the decline in the proportion of manual workers and rising levels of living have been accompanied, in the period since 1945, by a steady growth, in almost all the capitalist countries of Western Europe, in the membership of, and electoral support for, working-class parties, which are now stronger than ever before (in part because of the increased power of trade unions).[9] It can reasonably be argued, therefore, that one of the main tendencies in the development of capitalism during the present century has been the increasingly effective organization of workers as a class, engaged in a long-drawn-out class struggle, which takes the form, in democratic societies, of efforts to extend by degrees the sphere of social production and social provision and to limit the sphere of capitalist production and allocation of resources through the market. In this democratic class struggle there have been oscillations in the fortunes of different classes, and in Britain, for example, a major attempt has been made since 1979 to re-establish the predominance of the market, but the general tendency has been towards a more collective allocation of goods and services, and in many Western capitalist countries some 50 per cent of the gross domestic product (GDP) is now allocated in this way. These postwar developments themselves contributed to the rise in levels of living, through various forms of economic planning (and in particular the maintenance of full employment) and the extension of social services, including the provision of housing, health care and education on a greatly expanded scale.

But the political influence of the working class, although it has increased substantially, has been limited in various ways.[10] As I have suggested, the organization of workers as a class has been a long and difficult process, affected not only by the division between different categories of workers indicated by Adler (1933),[11] and by the major ideological and political division between communist and social democratic parties which emerged after 1917 and had as one of its most tragic consequences the rise to power of National Socialism in Germany, but by the advantages that the dominant class with which it is in conflict generally enjoys. We have also to consider, therefore, what consequences the development of capitalism has had for the power position of the bourgeoisie.

Schumpeter (1942), in his discussion of the 'decline of capitalism', although he did not explicitly conceive this process as the outcome of a conflict between classes, nevertheless argued that the disappearance of the entrepreneur 'affects the position of the entire bourgeois stratum [and] the perfectly bureaucratized giant industrial unit . . . . in the end . . . . ousts the entrepreneur and expropriates the bourgeoisie as a class' (p. 134). This tendency to undermine bourgeois dominance is reinforced, in his view, by the 'destruction of the protective strata' comprising those classes (the aristocracy and gentry, small traders, artisans and peasants) surviving from an earlier type of society (pp. 134–42), and by the increasing intervention of the state in economic life (p. 424). Schumpeter's general conception of capitalist development is that it passes through the three stages of entrepreneurial capitalism, organized or bureaucratic capitalism, and eventually socialism (or some 'halfway house') – a conception not unlike that which has been formulated, as we shall see, in some Marxist theories. Weber, on the other hand, writing during the period of revolutionary upheaval in Germany at the end of the First World War, clung to his conviction that 'the property-owning entrepreneurial bourgeoisie was the only group capable of providing the leadership to maintain a dynamic society' (Bahrdt, 1971). More generally, in his political sociology he argued, as did the elite theorists,[12] that in every society a dominant minority must rule, and this led him to the conclusion that the choice lay between the dominance of the bourgeoisie in a dynamic capitalist society and the 'dictatorship of the official' in an ossified socialist society.

In fact, the bourgeoisie has almost everywhere, except for very short periods, retained its dominance, and we have to consider how this has happened, despite the advances made by socialist parties during the twentieth century, and contrary to Schumpeter's expectations. Many factors, which can only be briefly indicated here, enter into this situation. In the first place, the bourgeoisie as an established dominant class enjoys the advantages of a long tradition of rule, education for and competence in this governing role, and command over economic resources and hence over some of the most important instruments for shaping opinion (in particular, newspapers and television). The growth of large corporations and state intervention in the economy have in many respects increased its resources, so that it has become more difficult to achieve the aim which Hilferding (1927) formulated as that of 'transforming an economy organized and directed by the *capitalists* into one which is directed by the *democratic state*'. In particular, the development of multinational corporations (the 'international centralization of capital') may, as Mandel (1975, pp. 326–9) argues, increase the power of the bourgeoisie on a world scale, either by an extension of the power of a single state (the USA), or by the rise of a new, federal, supranational bourgeois state power, which he suggests may be possible in the case of the European Economic Community. Undoubtedly the economic successes of capitalism (which Schumpeter emphasized for earlier periods) have also been a major factor since 1945, when, for three decades, they were greater than ever before; and, although this economic progress took place in the framework of a partly socialized economy (a 'managed economy' or 'mixed economy'), and to some extent under the influence of more powerful socialist parties, it did not by any means lead to the erosion of capitalist values which Schumpeter anticipated.[13] On the contrary, it may be argued that it is socialist values – the ideas of equality, co-operation, internationalism – that were slowly eroded during the postwar period of sustained economic growth, with the result that socialism and the working class no longer appear as the 'social head and heart' (to use Marx's phrase) of a movement of emancipation. Touraine (1980, pp. 11–12) has expressed this view in a radical way by saying that the word 'socialism' has become meaningless:

> Except when it refers to a vast family of authoritarian states
> . . . . Socialism was the theory of the labour movement; in a
> large part of the world it has become the name of the state
> power [while] in other countries it amounts only to a defence
> of particular sectional interests which are less and less the
> bearers of a general project of human progress.

At all events there has been over the past decade or so a vigorous bourgeois counter-offensive (which has taken a particularly extreme form in Britain), and the strength of the capitalist order seems to have increased rather than diminished over the whole postwar period.

This analysis suggests that the development of capitalism in the twentieth century has largely assured the continued dominance of the bourgeoisie, within the major capitalist countries and on a world scale: on one side by the massive accumulation and centralization of capital in large corporations and international banks, and by sustained, at times accelerating, economic growth; on the other side by the decline in socialist consciousness among large sections of the working class, whether this manifests itself as an outright rejection of socialism or as indifference and lack of commitment to any vision of a new form of society. It is in this context of the situation of other classes, and the relations between them, that the issue posed by Bernstein and continuously debated ever since – namely, the social and political significance to be attributed to the growth of the middle class – has to be examined.

This is an issue of daunting complexity, as the unceasing controversy itself reveals. Nevertheless, it is possible to identify some general characteristics of the middle class as it has developed in advanced capitalist societies, as the outcome of a transformation of the labour process through the advance of science and technology and the growth in size of enterprises (or centralization of capital), which Marx and Schumpeter both singled out as crucial features of capitalist development. First, what is broadly termed the 'middle class' comprises a great variety of different work and market situations. Abercrombie and Urry (1983), however, distinguish broadly between the 'service class'[14] and 'deskilled white-collar workers', and argue that while the service class 'is taking on, and concentrating within itself, the functions of capital', the deskilled white-collar workers are being proletarianized and 'cannot, therefore, be properly seen as a "middle class" '. But they go on to suggest that neither can the service class, since as a result of 'the depersonalization of property ownership, the distinctive market and work situation and hence class position of the capitalist class is being transformed, and its functions are becoming somewhat indistinguishable from those of the service class'; and they conclude that, because of the 'transformed relationship of labour and knowledge' in present-day capitalism, 'the process of class formation . . . . is increasingly the outcome of the distribution of hierarchically ordered educational credentials' (pp. 152–3). This is very close to the idea of the transformation of class structure in post-industrial society expounded by Touraine:

> The new ruling class can no longer be those who are in charge of and profit from private investment; it can only be all those who identify themselves with collective investment and who enter into conflict with those who demand increased consumption or whose private life resists change . . . . if property was the criterion of membership in the former dominant classes, the new dominant class is defined by knowledge and a certain level of education. (1971, pp. 47–51)

In short, after the rise of the middle class we are now witnessing its dissolution, and the emergence of a new dichotomous class structure, which Abercrombie and Urry, like Touraine, define by the separation of mental from manual labour, or of 'educated labour', concentrated in the increasingly dominant service class, from uneducated labour.

But this kind of argument dismisses too easily some persistent features of the class structure. It underestimates the continuing importance of the legal ownership of capital (and its close connection with effective 'possession'),[15] and the still considerable strength of the historically formed working-class movement, which I have briefly outlined above. At the same time it simplifies excessively the composition of the middle class by reducing it to two principal elements – the service class and the deskilled white collar workers – which are then treated as forming the core of a new class system. In reality, however, the middle class is extremely heterogeneous, and also very diverse in its political orientation. Different sections of the middle class – small shopkeepers and entrepreneurs, clerical workers, administrators and managers, professional people, teachers, intellectuals – show marked differences in their social and political attitudes, while even within these subgroups there is considerable diversity. Sections of the middle class have been, in particular historical situations, more or less conservative, fascist, liberal or socialist. Schumpeter, for example, considered that intellectuals were a major influence in creating a climate of hostility to capitalism; they had invaded and radicalized labour politics, 'eventually imparting a revolutionary bias to the most bourgeois trade union practices' (1942, p. 154).[16] On the other hand, electoral data and surveys of political attitudes indicate that over a long historical period a large part of the middle class (including intellectuals) has fairly consistently given its support to parties of the right or centre, and in some circumstances to fascist parties and military dictatorships.

There is, however, in the capitalist countries, a considerable mutability of middle-class political attitudes, and one major consequence of the growth of the middle class seems to have been a greater volatility in voting behaviour and a situation of stalemate between the two main classes. In this sense, the future development of capitalism depends in some degree upon how the balance of political commitment in the middle class evolves, but this in turn is strongly influenced by the extent to which the other classes are effectively organised, for as Brym (1980, p. 71) observes: '. . . . the relative power of fundamental classes (and other major groups) in a given time and place is often an important factor leading the middle strata in one direction or another'.

This relative power is itself affected by the development of the capitalist economy, and a second major element in Bernstein's revision of Marxism was his argument that crises were not growing worse, and, more generally, that capitalism was entering a phase of greater stability (Bernstein 1899, 1901). In the subsequent controversy, Kautsky (1899) criticized Bernstein for having wrongly attributed to Marx a theory of the eventual economic 'collapse' of capitalism, but went on to argue that crises were nevertheless 'becoming ever more severe and extensive in scope' (Kautsky, 1901–2).[17] As I noted earlier (see pp. 11–13 above) Marx himself did not provide a systematic theory of crises, but only partial analyses which do not embody a conception of the inevitable 'collapse' of capitalism; and in recent Marxist studies (e.g., Fine and Harris, 1979, Harvey, 1982) economic crises are conceived rather as violent restorations of equilibrium within a process of technological and organizational change which tends constantly to destabilize the economic system. This has some resemblance to Schumpeter's view of crises as 'gales of creative destruction' which periodically sweep over capitalism and continually infuse new life into it, through an upsurge of innovation and entrepreneurial dynamism. Schumpeter (1939) expounded this view in a very comprehensive and complex model of business cycles, in which he identified Kondratiev 'long waves' of about fifty years as a basic element and then distinguished within them shorter cycles of eight to nine years, and of forty months. More recently, the idea of 'long waves', caused by surges of new technology, has been incorporated into Marxist theory by Mandel (1975; see p. 13 above), but there has also been criticism of the whole idea of regular long-term changes in economic activity, notably by Maddison (1982), who suggests that the undoubted fluctuations in economic growth can best be explained by 'specific disturbances of an *ad hoc* character' (p. 83).[18]

Whether or not there are regular cycles in a capitalist economy which can be explained by reference to some general 'law', it is clearly the case that booms and depressions in economic activity occur, and the question that has now to be considered is what consequences these may have for the development of capitalism. Schumpeter, in his theory of the business cycle, treated it as one of the dynamic elements of capitalism, and was far from regarding economic crises as an indication of imminent decline or eventual collapse; on the contrary, capitalism would most probably perish as a result of the opposition engendered by its economic success. Weber, on the other hand (as I have shown in Chapter 2 above), paid little or no attention to the more recent features of capitalist development, and in *Economy and Society* he did not refer to crises at all. The Marxist theories are, as I have indicated, extremely diverse, ranging from ideas of economic 'collapse' or a 'general crisis' of capitalism (formulated in Bolshevik analyses of the 1930s) to conceptions which are in some respects close to Schumpeter's views, but differ from it fundamentally in the importance which they attribute to class relations. Thus Hilferding, in elaborating the notion of 'organized capitalism' (which may well have influenced Schumpeter's thought), insisted that the 'collapse of capitalism will be political and social, not economic', but he meant by this that it would be the outcome of a class struggle in which the working class would achieve political dominance.

In fact, it was in Hilferding's work, from *Finance Capital* (1910) to his essays and speeches of the 1930s, that a new Marxist theory of capitalist development took shape, differing greatly from that which was involved in the controversy around Bernstein's views. *Finance Capital* is concerned with three distinctive characteristics of the 'later phase of capitalist development' – the expansion of the credit system, the mobilization of capital through joint-stock companies and banks, and the restriction of free competition by the establishment of cartels and trusts – which Hilferding regards as being closely connected through the ever more intimate relationship between bank and industrial capital. From this analysis he proceeds to distinguish two main tendencies in the development of capitalism in the twentieth century. One is the emergence of an imperialist economic policy, in which the major elements are the formation of cartels, protective tariffs, the export of capital, and more generally the enlargement of the nation's 'economic territory' through an expansionist policy which requires a powerful nation state:

> Finance capital . . . . has no faith in the harmony of capitalist interests, and knows well that competition is becoming

increasingly a political power struggle . . . . The ideal now is to secure for one's own nation the domination of the world . . . .' (1910, p. 335).[19]

This was the main source of a Marxist theory of imperialism as a distinct stage of capitalism which was developed further, but in a somewhat different direction, by Bukharin (1918) and Lenin (1916). Bukharin's book (which Lenin read in manuscript before writing his own study) had *Finance Capital* as its 'starting point and essential inspiration' (Cohen, 1974, p. 25), but it presented the theory in a more intransigent way, arguing that finance capital could only pursue an imperialist policy leading inevitably to war, and depicting the process of capitalist development as one which passed necessarily from monopoly (finance) capitalism to imperialism, war and proletarian revolution. This was also Lenin's view, and it became an established tenet of Bolshevik doctrine during the First World War. Hilferding, however, did not regard war as an inevitable outcome of imperialist rivalries; working-class opposition, he thought, might check militarism and the preparations for war, and in so doing hasten the decline of capitalism. Later, in the 1920s, he argued that as a result of the economic dominance of the large corporations and banks, and growing state intervention in the economy, some degree of planning had spread into the international economy, so that the postwar relations between capitalist nation states had come to be characterized by what he called a 'realistic pacifism' (1924b).

Schumpeter was greatly influenced by Austro-Marxist thought, and in his early essay on imperialism (1919) he expresses a large measure of agreement with Hilferding's analysis:

> Thus we have here, within a social group [the entrepreneurs] that carries great political weight, a strong, undeniable, economic interest in such things as protective tariffs, cartels, monopoly prices, forced exports (dumping), an aggressive economic policy, an aggressive foreign policy generally, and war, including wars of expansion with a typically imperialist character. (p. 110)

At the same time, however, he argues that there are counter-vailing tendencies, and that imperialism is not a 'necessary stage of capitalism'. Hilferding, like Bukharin and Lenin, undoubtedly thought that it was; nevertheless, in his postwar writings he revised his views to some extent in recognizing that imperialist rivalries might become a less prominent feature of capitalist development, and that imperialism itself, in its colonialist form, might be a less permanent and less distinctive phenomenon than he had originally supposed. These ideas are very relevant to recent discussions, in which the significance of imperialism as an economic phenomenon, and in particular as a major phase of capitalist development, has appeared more questionable (see 'Colonialism' and 'Imperialism and world market' in Bottomore, 1983). The dissolution of colonial empires has brought important changes, and while the economic dominance of capitalism persists in much of the Third World, along with conflict among the major capitalist countries – notably between American, European and Japanese capitalism – the prospect of imperialist war as Bukharin or Lenin conceived it is remote, above all because of the overwhelming military superiority of the USA. On the other side, if the principal conflict of the present time, between the USA and the USSR, is to be regarded at all as a clash of empires engaged in a struggle for world supremacy it can only be so interpreted in terms of a broader, more political conception of imperialism as a phenomenon which has no specific relation with capitalism.

The second major tendency of capitalist development that Hilferding identified was the emergence of 'organized capitalism'. In the concluding chapter of *Finance Capital* he argues that:

> Finance capital puts control over social production increasingly into the hands of a small number of large capitalist associations, separates the management of production from ownership, and socializes production to the extent that this is possible under capitalism . . . . The socializing function of finance capital facilitates enormously the task of overcoming capitalism . . . . Even today, taking possession of six large Berlin banks would mean taking possession of the most important spheres of large-scale industry, and would greatly facilitate the initial phases of socialist policy during the transition period . . . . (pp. 367–8)

In his later writings, especially after the First World War, Hilferding elaborated this idea, and it is perhaps most fully expressed in a speech of 1927 (translated in Bottomore and Goode, 1983), where he characterizes the contemporary era as one in which 'we are moving . . . . from an economy regulated by the free play of forces to an organized economy' (p. 247). He then distinguishes four main features of this economy: first, its basis in technological progress (illustrated by the growth of the synthetic chemicals industry); second, the use of the new opportunities in an organized way, through cartels and trusts ('It is significant that newly-established industries are not only built upon a more complex technological base . . . . but at the same time are organizing themselves, so far as possible, on a world-wide scale'); third, the internationalization of capitalist industry; and, fourth, the replacement of free competition with scientific methods of planning (' . . . . organized capitalism means the theoretical replacement of the capitalist principle of free competition by the socialist principle of planned production') (pp. 247–9). The outcome is that 'this planned and consciously directed economy supports to a much greater extent the possibility of the conscious action of society', through the state.

Hilferding's general argument, that production is being socialized within the capitalist order itself,[20] was adopted by Schumpeter as the basis of his own conception; most of his argument about the development of capitalism, as he says, 'may be summed up in the Marxian proposition that the economic process tends to socialize *itself*' (1942, p. 219). Where his analysis diverges most widely from Marxist accounts (and particularly from the Austro-Marxist view) is in its treatment of the political concomitants of this economic process. In the first place, Schumpeter excludes completely the idea of class struggle as a fundamental element in the evolution of capitalist society. True, he identifies as a main feature of the decline of capitalism the fact that entrepreneurs and capitalists – indeed the whole bourgeois stratum – will eventually cease to function (p. 156), but it is, in his view, an ineluctable economic process that undermines the position of the bourgeoisie, and 'there is inherent in the capitalist system a tendency toward self-destruction' (p. 162). There is in

Schumpeter's theory a strongly marked, if largely implicit, economic determinism which is reminiscent of those nineteenth-century Marxist conceptions, now generally abandoned, of an inevitable economic 'collapse' of capitalism. At all events, the process of capitalist decline is not conceived as the outcome of a political struggle waged by an increasingly organized and powerful subordinate class. Of course, Schumpeter does pay attention to political movements, in the last section of his book dealing with the history of socialist parties (1976, pp. 305–406), but he explicitly rejects the idea that socialism is the doctrine and practice of a particular class, asserting that 'the labor movement is not essentially socialist, just as socialism is not necessarily laborite or proletarian'; and he goes on to say that this is not surprising, 'for we have seen . . . . that though the capitalist process slowly socializes economic life and much besides this spells transformation of the *whole* of the social organism *all* parts of which are equally affected' (p. 310). In so far as he considers any particular social group to be the 'bearer' of the process of socialization, and of a movement towards socialism, it is to the intellectuals rather than the working class that he assigns this role, and in this respect his thought can be related to some more recent studies;[21] but he does not pursue in any depth an analysis of the social groups involved in the transformation of modern capitalism.

After 1945 the socialization of the economy proceeded at a more rapid pace, and in Western Europe (but not in the USA or Japan) there was a more distinct movement towards socialism as the strength of working-class parties increased. The economic dominance of large corporations continued to grow, the internationalization of capitalist production went on apace with the development of multinational corporations, and the economic role of the state was steadily enhanced by the expansion of public services and the nationalization of some sectors of the economy. To this extent the predictions of the Austro-Marxists and Schumpeter have been confirmed, and in recent Marxist thought these postwar developments have given renewed interest and prominence to the theory of 'organized capitalism', even though the ideas embodied in it may sometimes be expressed in other terms. Thus, the theory of 'state monopoly capitalism' which has been elaborated by Marxist economists in the USSR, the German Democratic Republic, and to some extent in France, over the past two decades, incorporates virtually the same ideas as Hilferding originally expounded – the dominance of large corporations arising from the centralization and concentration of capital, growing state intervention and as a consequence a more extensive socialization of the economy (which constitutes the basis for a transition to socialism) and a relative stabilization of capitalism – but as befits a more 'orthodox' Marxist outlook it is set firmly in the framework of the long-established Bolshevik conception of a 'general crisis of capitalism', even if this crisis is now treated as being only a 'latent' instability, and is neither rigorously analysed nor related to any actual political movements in present-day capitalist societies.[22] Whether 'organized capitalism' in Hilferding's or Schumpeter's sense can be regarded today as a stage on the road to socialism is a question I shall consider in the next chapter.

The conceptions of capitalist development propounded by Weber and by Hayek can be considered together in so far as both thinkers are primarily and specifically concerned with the dangers that beset the freedom and autonomy of the individual in the conditions of modern society. Their ways of approaching this question are, however, very different. For Weber, individual autonomy is already profoundly threatened by the development of industrial capitalism, through the rationalization of administration (bureaucracy) and production (mechanization), and what he calls the 'inexorable power of material goods' (or, in modern parlance, the ubiquitous influence of 'consumerism') – all of which, in his view, tend to reduce the human being to the condition of a 'cog in a machine', with no other ambition than to become a somewhat larger cog.[23] One of his major criticisms of socialism[24] is simply that it will accelerate this process: '. . . . assuming that [the elimination of private capitalism] eventually happens, what would that mean in practice? The destruction of the iron cage of modern industrial labour? No! Rather that the administration of nationalized or "socialized" enterprises too would become bureaucratic [and] the state bureaucracy would rule *alone*' (1924, pp. 331–2). Hayek, on the other hand, as I have shown in the preceding chapter, does not examine the actual development of industrial capitalism and its consequences, but establishes a contrast between an ideal version of capitalism, which is equated with human freedom (narrowly conceived as market freedom), and a grim depiction of socialism as 'serfdom' or 'totalitarianism'.

Nevertheless, the same kind of question can be addressed to both Weber and Hayek: namely, whether the progressive rationalization and socialization of the economy – the uninterrupted advance of technology and mechanization of production, the growing dominance of large, bureaucratically managed corporations, the increasing intervention of the state – have diminished, or on the contrary enlarged, the sphere of individual freedom. Weber is a better guide than Hayek in examining this issue, because he has a broader, less economistic conception of the diverse elements that go to constitute individual autonomy, close to existentialism in its emphasis upon moral choice and responsibility (Brubaker, 1984, ch. 4), and as a sociologist is more aware of the differential impact of these processes upon different social groups; but his analysis is still strongly influenced by his own value preferences (which, as he freely confessed,[25] were those of the 'bourgeois class'), formed in part by the powerful current in German social thought from the end of the nineteenth century which expressed hostility to science and technology and aimed to reassert 'spiritual' values.[26] It is no doubt exceedingly difficult, if at all possible, to draw up an exact historical balance sheet of the gains and losses in individual liberty during the twentieth century, but it can be asserted with some confidence that rationalization and socialization have not brought unmitigated loss. Against the rationalization of the labour process, bureaucratic administration, and a greater degree of state regulation (in some areas, but by no means in all, for we live, after all, in 'permissive societies') we must set the consequences, for very large numbers of people, of higher levels of living, more leisure time, full employment (when there *was* full employment) and greater economic security in general, better health care, and improved educational opportunities – all of which have greatly enlarged the realm of individual choice and self-determination. We should also take account of the fact that industrial employment, which Weber saw as particularly affected by mechanization, has steadily declined, from which it may be argued that the scientific and technological revolution in production has on the whole resulted in a movement from more routine and irksome jobs to those which are more interesting, require greater initiative (and a higher level of education), and allow the individual more freedom of choice in the execution of the work.[27]

This enlargement of freedom for vast numbers of people in the societies of Western Europe has taken place, since 1945, in the context of increasing rationalization and socialization, with the latter, in some periods, assuming the conscious form of a movement towards socialism. We have now to consider, in the next chapter, whether this process of socialization is still continuing, whether what is emerging is, as Schumpeter thought, socialism, or perhaps a new type of capitalism, and what consequences, in the future, this process might have for the individual.

NOTES TO CHAPTER 5

1 The major early consideration of his view of the developmental tendencies of capitalism is the monograph by Löwith (1932).
2 For a good recent account see Marshall, 1982.
3 See the study of Bernstein by Gay, 1952, especially Chapter 7 and pp. 244–7.
4 See, for example, the conclusions reached by Abercrombie and Urry, 1983.
5 There is a comprehensive assessment of recent analyses of the middle classes in Abercrombie and Urry, 1983. For a discussion of conceptions of the working class and its place in the class structure see my essays 'Class and politics in Western Europe' (Bottomore, 1975), 'Socialism and the working class' and 'The political role of the working class in Western Europe' (Bottomore, 1984a); and also the extensive discussion by Przeworski, 1977.
6 Some of these issues, moreover, were already raised by Marx and Engels themselves, in their brief references to the growth of the middle classes and the emergence of a 'labour aristocracy'.
7 For a detailed account of the changes in Britain from 1911 to 1971, and some international comparisons, see Routh, 1980, ch. 1.
8 See Maddison, 1982, p. 115, where the average of 16 countries is presented.
9 See my discussion in Bottomore, 1984a, ch. 11.
10 It also varies considerably between countries, and a comprehensive analysis, such as cannot be undertaken here, would have to explore thoroughly the nature of the economic and cultural differences, and the historical traditions associated with them, which have produced these variations – for example, between the USA or Japan and Europe, or within Europe between France or Sweden and Britain. On the peculiarities of the American experience see

especially Sombart, 1906, and the introduction to the English translation, 1976.

11 See also the discussion by Hilferding (1941) of 'the most difficult problem' of 'the relation between *class interests* and class *consciousness*', and of the fact that 'nowhere has *socialist* consciousness taken hold of the entire working class'.

12 See Bottomore, 1964.

13 See my discussion in Bottomore, 1984a, pp. 147–55.

14 The term 'service class' was first used by Renner (1953) in his analysis of the changing character of capitalism in the twentieth century. But he conceived the service class in quite a different way, as comprising the managers and officials both in the capitalist economic sphere and in the public service, who had formerly had some of the characteristics of a caste, but now form a class, which is largely propertyless, and 'is closer to the rising working class in its life style, and at its boundary tends to merge with it.'

15 See the discussion, in relation to joint-stock companies, by Mandel (in Bottomore, 1983), and the general analysis of property relations by Hegedüs (1976, pp. 93–105).

16 But this exaggerates both the radicalism and the influence of intellectuals in modern capitalist societies. For a good analysis of the diverse political commitments of intellectuals, see Brym, 1980.

17 For an account of the controversy about the 'collapse' or 'breakdown' of capitalism, see Gay, 1952, pp. 176–190, Sweezy, 1942, pp. 190–213, and Kühne 1979, Vol. 2, pp. 181–234, 261–296.

18 Maddison also provides a useful summary of the different 'cycle' or 'crisis' theories (1982, pp. 64–95). It may be noted that Schumpeter too, while he formulated a cycle theory, explained the severity of the 1929–33 depression in terms of specific influences and mistakes of policy. See also Freeman, 1983, especially ch. 1.

19 This, it may be noted, is the idea expressed, though in a muted form, in Weber's writings on the nation state. See Bottomore, 1984a, ch. 7.

20 This process had already been briefly outlined by Marx – for example, in *Capital*, Vol. 3, where he observes that 'the joint-stock companies in general . . . . have a tendency to separate the function of management more and more from the ownership of capital' (ch. 23) and represent 'the abolition of the capitalist mode of production within capitalist production itself' (ch. 27); and in the *Grundrisse* (pp. 704–6), where he emphasizes the importance, in the development of large-scale industry, of the 'objectified power of knowledge' and continues: 'The development of fixed capital indicates the extent to which general social knowledge has become a *direct force of production*, and thus the extent to which the conditions of the social life process have been brought under the control of the general intellect.' Subsequently, Karl Renner (like Hilferding a leading thinker of the Austro-Marxist school) emphasized, as another major aspect of this socialization of the economy, the growth of state intervention, 'the penetration of the private economy down to its elementary cells by the state [and] the control of the whole private sector of the economy by willed and conscious regulation and direction . . . . The enterprise takes the place of the entrepreneur and becomes semi-public' (Renner, 1916).

21 See especially Konrád and Szelényi, 1979. See also Lasswell (in Lasswell and Lerner, 1965, p. 85), who argues that 'the major transformation is the

decline of business (and of earlier social formations) and the rise of intellectuals and semi-intellectuals to effective power', attributing the original formulation of this view to Machajski (1905); and on the general relation of intellectuals to politics, Brym, 1980.

22 See the exposition of the theory in Wirth, 1972, and critical evaluations in Hardach and Karras, 1978, and Jessop, 1982.

23 See the discussion in Löwith, 1932. Hilferding (1910, p. 347), examining the phenomenon of bureaucratization from a different perspective, also observes that the growth of salaried employment has created a new hierarchical system, which in his view helps to sustain the bourgeois social order.

24 His other main criticism was that a socialist economy would be deprived of the means of rational calculation in so far as it involved physical allocation of resources rather than the use of money and a price mechanism.

25 In his inaugural lecture at the University of Freiburg (1895).

26 For a general account, see the discussion of the 'revolt against positivism' in Hughes, 1958, ch. 2.

27 Various aspects of these changes are examined in Bottomore, 1984a, ch. 9.

6

From Capitalism
to Socialism?

Towards the end of the First World War, Mommsen (1974, p. 58) notes, 'many people in Germany discussed whether the state-controlled war economy would gradually lead to a socialist system'.[1] In this debate Weber took the view that while the elimination of private capitalism is 'theoretically possible . . . . it will certainly not be brought about by the present war' (Weber, 1918a). A quarter of a century later, in the Second World War, Schumpeter was arguing that the 'march into socialism' is well under way and 'a socialist form of society will inevitably emerge from an equally inevitable decomposition of capitalist society' (1942, p. 409),[2] while Hayek (1944) similarly drew attention to the strength of the movement towards socialism and uttered a shrill warning against the ultimate consequences of following this 'road to serfdom'. These accounts are all related, in one way or another, to Marx's theory of capitalist development, which – it has generally been held – asserts the *necessity* of a transition to socialism, determined by the contradictions within capitalism itself.[3] We have now to consider how far the economic, social and political changes of the twentieth century in Western societies do manifest, if not an ineluctable process of transition to a socialist society, at least a general tendency towards that end.

In his lecture on socialism (1918b) Weber formulates several criticisms of the Marxist theory of capitalist decline. First, he rejects the 'pauperization thesis', which he interprets, however, in a rather eccentric manner as asserting that there will be an ever-increasing 'industrial reserve army' of the permanently unemployed, of paupers, and that at some point this will make capitalist society unviable. He goes on to say that this view has now been abandoned by Marxists, but in fact it was never a part of Marx's theory, and it is worthy of note that Weber's whole discussion of Marxism is based upon an interpretation of a few passages in the *Communist Manifesto* (supplemented by occasional references to Kautsky) without any attention to Marx's theoretical writings.[4]

Second, Weber criticizes the Marxist view of the social consequences of the centralization and concentration of capital – namely, a diminishing number of large capitalists and an increase in the size of the working class – which he expresses in his own way as the thesis that 'at some time the number of these entrepreneurs will have contracted so much that it will be impossible for them to maintain their domination'. Against this view Weber argues (as did Bernstein) that the process of concentration is not occurring everywhere, e.g., in agriculture (but in the longer term he was obviously mistaken about this), and further that the concentration of capital in large corporations is accompanied by a rapid increase in the number of clerical workers (i.e. by the growth of private bureaucracy), whose interests 'do not lie unequivocally in the direction of a proletarian dictatorship'. He goes on to suggest that the emergence of very complex and diverse interests in this process of capitalist development makes it impossible to assert, at the present time, that the numbers and power of those who are directly or indirectly interested in maintaining the bourgeois order are diminishing. This argument has clearly remained important in the debate about the future of capitalism.

Finally, Weber claims (again in close agreement with Bernstein's ideas)[5] that economic crises have diminished in importance with the partial elimination of competition through the formation of trusts and cartels and the regulation of the credit system by the banks, so that there is now much less likelihood of a revolutionary upheaval arising out of such crises. His general conclusion from the foregoing arguments is that 'the very high hopes which were placed in a collapse of bourgeois society in the *Communist Manifesto* have therefore been replaced by far more sober expectations', and he goes on to discuss the emergence of an 'evolutionary socialism', in which the main themes are the gradual socialization of production, the greater homogeneity of the working class brought about by the mechanization of production, and the increasing standardization of production which tends to eliminate the entrepreneur and substitute a bureaucratic administration of productive enterprises.

These themes, and above all the idea of a gradual socialization of the economy, have remained prominent in all later discussions. But what precisely is meant by this process of socialization? In Marx's brief comments on the subject it is portrayed in two forms: as the rise of the joint-stock company and the replacement of the individual entrepreneur by the industrial 'manager'; and as the increasing dependence of production upon the growth of 'social knowledge' in the domain of science and technology. Subsequently, in the writings of Hilferding and Schumpeter, the joint-stock company is seen as the crucial factor in an accelerating centralization of capital in large corporations, a transition from competitive capitalism to monopoly capitalism, and the emergence of a partially 'planned economy'. Along with this development, it may be argued, the labour process itself has been transformed, from one in which the skills of individual workers were supremely important, through a phase of assembly-line production, to a phase of 'social rationalization' in which the essential feature is the interdependence of all those engaged in production, at whatever level, within the framework of a planned technical organization of labour. Touraine, for example, having presented an analysis along these lines (1965, ch. 5), has gone on to propound the view that modern societies have come increasingly to recognize themselves as 'the product of their labour and their social relations . . . . the result of a social action, of decisions or transactions, of domination or conflicts', and as being engaged in a continuous process of 'self-production' (Touraine, 1977).

A second major element in the idea of a progressive socialization of the economy is the growth of state intervention, which was emphasized by Renner (1916), considered briefly by Weber (1918b) – who, however, argued that a continuation of the state control of industry established during the war would be disastrous in peacetime – and is a principal feature in the analyses of Hilferding and Schumpeter as well as in the theory of state monopoly capitalism. But increased state intervention can take diverse forms and have various outcomes. In a general sense, no doubt, it tends to diffuse more widely an awareness that the economy is a *social* enterprise, and that the level and direction of economic activity in an advanced industrial society depends crucially upon political decisions. At the same time, as state intervention increases it brings into existence the instruments, organizations, and procedures which are required for an effective social regulation of economic life. But it does not follow that the activities of the state, however much they, in conjunction with the development of large-scale enterprises, establish some of the preconditions for a socialist society, necessarily lead towards socialism. Other tendencies are possible – towards a corporate economy,[6] a totalitarian state economy,[7] a new type of capitalism,[8] or even a restoration of old-style capitalism[9] – depending upon which class or social group controls the state power.

The extent of state intervention also raises another question, about the consequences of the growth in state power as such, which is examined most directly, within Marxist thought, by Hilferding in his later writings, while it constitutes a central concern of Weber, and more particularly of Hayek. In Hilferding's work (1940, 1941) the problem of the state as an independent power arose in the first place out of his experience of the National Socialist regime in Germany, but his analysis is also directed upon the nature of Soviet society, and he arrives at the general conclusion that Marx's theory of history needs to be revised to take account of the fact that:

> the political superstructure of society is a power in its own right, with its own agencies, its own tendencies and its own interests. The development of *state power* accompanies the development of the modern economy . . . . The political problem of the postwar period consists in the change in the relation of the state to society, brought about by the *subordination of the economy* to the coercive power of the state . . . . The subordination of all historically significant social processes to the consciousness of the state, to the conscious will of the state, means the suppression of those areas of social life which previously were free from state

influence and were regulated by autonomous laws. (1941)

Weber, for his part, identified the tendency towards greater state power with the movement towards socialism, claiming that 'if private capitalism were eliminated the state bureaucracy would rule *alone*' and that the general course of social development was leading much more obviously to a 'dictatorship of the official' than to a 'dictatorship of the proletariat' (1918a); and the same theme has been developed at length by Hayek, who proposes, in order to safeguard individual liberty, a drastic curtailment of the powers of the state.

But the relation between the growth of state power and an assumed 'march into socialism' is more complex than some of these accounts suggest. In the first place, it is necessary to distinguish between 'bureaucratic power' and 'political power'. Weber was concerned above all with the former – the 'dictatorship of the official'[10] – but Schumpeter, as we have seen (pp. 40–1 above), thought that bureaucracy was not only compatible with, but essential to, a democratic system of government. Nevertheless, there has undoubtedly emerged in modern societies some resentment of, and opposition to, the extension of state regulation, though it should be noted that this is not directed specifically against more socialist forms of regulation, and that there is, on the other side, a strong desire for the services which the state provides. More important is the fact that the authoritarian states of the twentieth century have been characterized not by bureaucratic domination but by the domination of a political party which has eliminated all its rivals, or in some cases by a military diitatorship. In less extreme forms there is an evident tendency towards increasing the power of the centralized state, in order to control dissent and opposition, especially in periods of economic crisis, even in societies whose governments claim to be dedicated to extending individual freedom – as is the case, for example, in present-day Britain. Finally, the power of the state, as the political executive (i.e. government), has increased not only with the development of the modern economy, as Hilferding argued, but with the growing rivalry between nation states. During much of the twentieth century capitalist states (and more recently other kinds of regime) have been organised on a semi-war footing, and this has greatly enhanced the power of the state. The crucial question,[11] then, is not that of combating bureaucratic domination, although democratic control over officials is in itself important, but of controlling political leaders and governments in a democratic regime; and there is no compelling reason to suppose that this would necessarily be more difficult under socialism than under capitalism.[12]

The process of socialization – however diverse the ways in which its eventual outcome is portrayed or judged – is presented in some of the theories I have considered as an impersonal, more or less irresistible, tendency which resembles in this respect the processes of 'rationalization' and 'bureaucratization' that Weber saw as the inescapable 'fate of our time'. In Marxist thought this idea has usually been expressed in some kind of 'collapse' theory, according to which the end of capitalism will follow necessarily from its own economic contradictions, manifested in ever-worsening crises. This kind of theory does not seem to be widely held by present-day Marxist thinkers (and as I indicated in Chapter 1 it has an insecure basis in Marx's own analysis of crises), although elements of it can be found in some modern versions of Marxism. Thus Sweezy (1972) argues that under the conditions of monopoly capitalism accumulation is retarded while the 'economic surplus' continues to increase, with the result that there are 'ever more powerful tendencies to stagnation', only partially counteracted by the expansion of 'socially wasteful' expenditure (e.g., on marketing, and above all on the arms race).[13] From a different perspective the structuralist Marxists[14] have also emphasized the necessary character of the transition from capitalism to socialism, determined by 'structural contradictions'; and Godelier (1972), for example, argues that:

> the *structure* of socialist relations of production *corresponds* functionally with the conditions of rapid development of the new, gigantic, more and more socialized productive forces created by capitalism . . . . this correspondence is totally *independent* of any a priori idea of happiness, of 'true liberty', of the essence of man, etc. Marx demonstrates the necessity and superiority of a new mode of production . . . . (p. 354)

Schumpeter's account of the decline of capitalism has some affinities with a 'collapse' theory, although in this case it is no longer a matter of economic collapse. In the preface to the first edition of *Capitalism, Socialism and Democracy*, as I noted earlier, he spoke indeed of 'an inevitable decomposition of capitalist society', and while this view was heavily qualified later on his analysis still emphasizes the determinism of a process in which the economy tends to 'socialize itself'. Of course, socialization is conceived as being brought about, in a formal sense, by socialist governments, but their activities are not related to the interests, values and actions of social groups (and notably of classes) except to the extent that Schumpeter seems to regard the intellectuals as the principal source of the whole socialist movement (see p. 39 above).

Such analyses are, in my view, insufficient to account fully for the processes of social change. Any transformation of a society (or, equally, its maintenance in a given form) involves the conscious actions – a series of conscious actions – of individuals who are associated in groups of diverse kinds. As Marx wrote, 'human beings make their own history'. He went on to observe, however, that 'they do not make it just as they please . . . . under circumstances chosen by themselves, but under circumstances directly encountered, given and transmitted from the past' (*Eighteenth Brumaire*). There are, that is to say, degrees of determination in social life, but what is involved is not a mechanical determinism in which effects flow from their causes in an impersonal, unconscious, and strictly necessitated sequence of events; it is rather one that is mediated by consciousness – a quasi-causality[15] – in terms of which social laws have to be conceived as stating tendencies and limits, not as prescribing uniquely fixed results.[16]

From this perspective the movement towards socialism must be seen as the outcome of tendencies that develop within capitalist society – economic contradictions and crises, the centralization of capital, state intervention, the opposition of class interests – which are modified and given a political significance by conscious choices and decisions, but in a context which these tendencies themselves have produced. Let us consider in these terms the effects of economic crises. Bernstein's (and Weber's) claim that economic crises were not becoming worse was controverted by the experience of the Great Depression of 1929–33. This did not lead to a 'collapse', but it undoubtedly weakened capitalism, which could only be maintained in some countries (e.g., Germany) by extreme violence and the establishment of a dictatorial regime, while elsewhere a greater degree of planning and state regulation of the economy was introduced. In the longer term the experience of the 1930s strengthened the socialist movement and led to the postwar policies of full employment, the welfare state, and the nationalization of basic industries. I think it is probable that the present economic crisis will ultimately have a similar outcome, for among its consequences are likely to be a political radicalization of the labour movement and a more general movement of opinion towards the idea of a more fully socialized economy. In this context the 'long waves' which both Schumpeter and Mandel (from different theoretical positions) treat as a major feature of capitalist development may, if their analysis is correct,[17] have considerable significance, for it could then be argued that after every serious crisis, occurring at regular intervals of about fifty years, a further socialization of the economy is consciously and deliberately undertaken, at a higher level than that which was achieved on the preceding occasion.

I shall consider in a moment what other conditions are necessary for this to happen, but first it is necessary to say something about the time scale involved in any conception of the stages of capitalist development and of a possible transition to socialism. Marx, and later social historians, all recognize that the transition from feudalism to capitalism in Western Europe was a lengthy, irregular and complex process, spread over several centuries,[18] in which different phases are distinguishable. Is there any reason to suppose that a transition from capitalism to socialism will be more rapid or less complex? Marx himself, in his writings on current politics, sometimes conveys the impression that he expected the advent of a socialist society in the very near future, but this is not altogether consistent with the analysis of capitalist development in his theoretical writings. On the other hand, the rapid growth of the socialist movement in Germany at the end of the nineteenth century led Engels, in the last years of his life, to anticipate, not unreasonably, a decisive advance towards socialism there – a view that was shared by Hilferding and others in the first decade of the twentieth century. In the event their expectations were disappointed. Nevertheless, it was *possible* that a socialist society should emerge in Germany, and over a large area of Central Europe, in the years immediately after the First World War; and if that had happened the course of European and world history would evidently have been very different from that which actually resulted from the Russian Revolution, the destruction of the Weimar Republic and the rise of National Socialism. But the failure of the Central European revolutions and the absence of revolutionary movements elsewhere, as well as the subsequent experience of the economic depression, may also be taken to indicate the continuing strength of capitalism, and the relative weakness of the socialist movement, during the first half of the twentieth century. It is only since 1945, as I suggested earlier (p. 57 above), that socialism has become a really powerful force in Western Europe, while at the same time its advance has provoked a vigorous debate about the nature of a socialist society – how its economy would be organized, what form its social institutions would take, what changes in the mode of life would emerge – in the context of an outright rejection of the model of authoritarian socialism which prevails in much of Eastern Europe.

If the movement towards socialism is conceived in this way, as a long-term process, then another similarity with the rise of capitalism becomes apparent; for just as in that earlier transition the developing capitalist mode of production coexisted for a time with elements of the preceding feudal mode of production, so it may be argued that in present-day Western societies (and still more on a world scale) there is a coexistence of the still dominant capitalist mode with a new socialist mode of production. This is what might be meant by a 'mixed economy', or by a situation such as Schumpeter indicated in which the 'march into socialism' comes to a halt at some kind of 'halfway house'. Most of the West European societies now seem to be roughly equally divided politically between those who desire to extend the socialization of the economy (but not necessarily to the culminating point of a distinctively socialist society, which in any case may be only dimly visualized) and those who wish to maintain some kind of 'mixed economy' or to revert to a more *laissez-faire*, free-market economy (either of which means in effect the continuing dominance of private capital). This balance of forces, which some studies of advanced capitalism (e.g., Habermas, 1976) have interpreted in terms of a 'class compromise' reached during the period of rapid economic growth in the 1950s and 1960s, has been expressed in the 'consensus politics' of the past two or three decades, but it seems doubtful that it will survive the present economic crisis. Class conflict is now becoming more intense, and whatever the immediate consequences of the crisis its eventual outcome may be a strengthening of the movement towards a more predominantly socialist, planned economy, above all in order to combat mass unemployment and the deterioration of public services.

Any further advance towards socialism depends crucially, however, upon the ability of a political party (or alliance of parties) representing the working class to express a vision of the new society that will arouse the enthusiasm not only of the great majority of members of that class but also of other sections of society whose interests and aspirations are frustrated by the existing social order. In short, it must be able to diffuse widely through society a socialist consciousness, as working-class parties in the Western world have so far succeeded in doing only for short periods of time and in exceptional conditions.[19] This requirement brings to light a significant difference between the transition to socialism and previous historical transformations, which were accomplished in less deliberate ways. The early capitalist entrepreneurs were not consciously attempting to bring into existence a 'capitalist society'. They were pursuing their own economic interests in an environment shaped by many different circumstances – the advance of science and technology, the growth of towns and nation states, the expansion of trade, the spread of a 'calculating' attitude and of a view of economic activity as a God-given 'calling' – which made possible the development of the capitalist mode of production. In that sense they did produce a result which was 'no part of their intention' – a 'spontaneous order', as Hayek would call it – although at a later stage, in the political struggles of the seventeenth and eighteenth centuries against the *ancien régime*, a distinct idea of 'bourgeois society', characterized by greater individual freedom and endowed with new institutions, came to be formulated in the theories and doctrines of philosophers, economists and historians.

By contrast, the working-class movement was imbued from the outset with the idea of a future form of society which was to be consciously and deliberately constructed. To that extent Schumpeter's view of the importance of intellectuals in the socialist movement (if purged of some exaggerations) is warranted, as is the distinctively Marxist conception of the relation between theory and practice in that movement, in which there is interaction between conceptions of a future socialist society and the actual life experiences of a subordinate class. It was the working-class movement which brought into existence mass political parties, and along with them a great extension of political education and an entirely new intensity of political controversy, with the result that the future of capitalism has come to depend, in an unprecedented degree, upon the outcome of ideological confrontations. The intellectual defence of capitalism, in the closing decades of the twentieth century, rests upon claims about its economic efficiency, but still more – in the writings of Hayek and the 'new right' – upon the identification of market freedom with human freedom in general, and the contrast which can be drawn with the authoritarian socialism of Eastern Europe; while the criticism of it centres upon what Weber termed its 'substantive irrationality' – the subordination and injustice which it entails – and upon the hopes of greater equality and community, and more complete human emancipation, that are held out by socialist doctrine. In this contestation the vigour of the socialist idea, notwithstanding the growth of socialist parties, has undoubtedly declined over the past few decades, confronted with the reality of 'actually existing socialism' and deprived of the experience of a functioning socialist society in which the primordial aims of socialism are more fully realized. Some radical thinkers have declared the idea dead or dying, while many others recognize that socialist thought and socialist movements have been, and are still, passing through a period of crisis. Nevertheless, the idea continually re-emerges, assuming new forms, and it remains a powerful influence upon the development of Western societies.

What then can be concluded about the likely outcome of the conflict between capitalism and socialism as alternative ways of organizing economic life and social relations? I do not think it is possible to predict with any great assurance the course of events even for the medium-term future (a period of about forty years in Schumpeter's sense), but only to distinguish, as I have attempted to do, the main tendencies and their possible results. There is, unmistakably, an on-going process of socialization of the economy, which manifests itself in the continued growth of large-scale enterprises, and of state intervention and planning to provide the infrastructure of knowledge required in modern production, to manage demand, to sustain the national economy in the competitive struggle with other nations (which also involves the direction of investment into vital sectors), and to ensure a minimum level of consensus and social cohesion by means of welfare policies. This real process of socialization is accompanied by a growing conscious recognition of the social character of production, which may ultimately lead to some conception of the 'self-production' of society as a whole. Further, within this process of socialization, as an integral part of it, there is the struggle of a subordinate class – the working class – to emancipate itself and to participate fully in the organization of social life. And, finally, these tendencies are expressed in the opposing political doctrines of conservatism and socialism, upon whose success or failure in mobilizing opinion and action the actual course of events will mainly depend.

NOTES TO CHAPTER 6

1 This was also a major element, for instance in Renner's (1916) analysis of the socialization of the economy (see p. 72 above).

2 Schumpeter's forthright prediction, in his preface to the first edition of the book, was qualified in later editions, and he then referred to 'observable tendencies' towards socialism (1976, p. 422; see also p. 54 above).

3 As we shall see, however, the degree of 'determination' is a matter of controversy among Marxist thinkers, influenced by different conceptions of what are the major contradictions.

4 It is clear that Weber had a very limited, almost entirely second-hand, knowledge of Marx's work. On the specific question of 'pauperization' see the entry in Bottomore, 1983.

5   The whole of this part of Weber's lecture can and should be read as a restatement of Bernstein's arguments.

6   See Panitch, 1980, and the model of advanced capitalism outlined by Habermas, 1976.

7   See Neumann, 1944, and Hilferding's later writings which are discussed in the text below.

8   As one critic of Schumpeter's theory has suggested. See the essay by Fellner in Heertje, 1981, pp. 66–7, and the earlier discussion in Tsuru, 1961.

9   This seems to be the aim of the present British government which, in order to restore the profitability of capital, is undertaking a massive re-privatisation of the economy while pursuing a general economic policy which creates very high unemployment and hence strong pressures to reduce wage levels.

10 His concern was provoked in large measure by the specific conditions that existed in post-Bismarck Germany, as his writings on German politics show very clearly. See especially Weber, 1918a.

11 Leaving aside here the problem posed by international rivalries, which would require an extensive separate analysis. It is clear, as I have noted in the text, that militarism and war tend to increase state power, and that the opportunities for diminishing this power would be greater in a more peaceful world.

12 But it would still not be easy, as the experience of the 'actually existing' socialist countries demonstrates, and the question of effective democratic institutions in a socialist society remains acutely controversial.

13 It is worth noting in this connection that the economic recovery from the depression of the 1930s only became significant when the major capitalist countries began to rearm; and of course this was most evident in Germany under the National Socialist regime.

14 For a brief account of their ideas, see 'Structuralism' in Bottomore, 1983.

15 See the discussion in von Wright, 1971, ch. 4.

16 See 'Determinism', in Bottomore, 1983.

17 But see the criticisms by Maddison, p. 63 above, and also Freeman, 1983.

18 At least from the fifteenth to the eighteenth century, as portrayed in Braudel's massive study (1981–4).

19 For example, the British Labour Party, in the election of 1945, gained not only its largest ever working-class support but also its largest share of middle-class support.

Bibliography

Note: In the case of works by Marx and Engels details of the English publication are not generally given, since various translations are available.

Abercrombie, Nicholas, and Urry, John (1983), *Capital, Labour and the Middle Classes* (London: Allen & Unwin).

Adler, Max (1933), 'Metamorphosis of the working class', in Bottomore and Goode, 1978.

Aron, Raymond (1967a), *18 Lectures on Industrial Society* (London: Weidenfeld & Nicolson).

Aron, Raymond (1967b), *The Industrial Society* (London: Weidenfeld & Nicolson).

Bahrdt, H. P. (1971), 'Contribution to discussion on "Max Weber and power politics" ', in Otto Stammer (ed.), *Max Weber and Sociology Today* (Oxford: Basil Blackwell).

Bauer, Otto (1907), *Die Nationalitätenfrage und die Sozialdemokratie* (Vienna: Wiener Volksbuchhandlung, 2nd enlarged edn. 1924).

Bernstein, Eduard (1899), *Evolutionary Socialism* (New York: Schocken Books, 1961).

Bernstein, Eduard (1901), *Zur Geschichte und Theorie des Sozialismus* (Berlin: Edelheim).

Bottomore, Tom (1964), *Elites and Society* (Harmondsworth: Penguin Books, 1966).

Bottomore, Tom (1965), *Classes in Modern Society* (London: Allen & Unwin).

Bottomore, Tom (1976), 'Introduction' to Schumpeter, *Capitalism, Socialism and Democracy*, 5th edn.

Bottomore, Tom (ed.) (1981), *Modern Interpretations of Marx* (Oxford: Basil Blackwell).

Bottomore, Tom (ed.) (1983), *A Dictionary of Marxist Thought* (Oxford: Basil Blackwell).

Bottomore, Tom (1984a), *Sociology and Socialism* (Brighton: Harvester Press).

Bottomore, Tom (1984b), *The Frankfurt School* (Chichester and London: Ellis Horwood/Tavistock).

Bottomore, Tom, and Goode, Patrick (eds) (1983), *Readings in Marxist Sociology* (Oxford: Clarendon Press).

Braudel, Fernand (1981–4), *Civilization and Capitalism, 15th–18th Century* (3 vols) (London: Collins).

Braverman, Harry (1974), *Labour and Monopoly Capitalism: The Degradation of Work in the Twentieth Century* (New York: Monthly Review Press).

Bronfenbrenner, Martin (1965), '*Das Kapital* for the modern man', *Science and Society*, Autumn 1965; repr. in David Horowitz (ed.), *Marx and Modern Economics* (London: MacGibbon & Kee, 1968).

Brubaker, Rogers (1984), *The Limits of Rationality: An Essay on the Social and Moral Thought of Max Weber* (London: Allen & Unwin).

Brym, Robert J. (1980), *Intellectuals and Politics* (London: Allen & Unwin).

Bukharin, Nikolai (1918), *Imperialism and World Economy* (London: Merlin Press, 1972).

Carchedi, Guglielmo (1977), *On the Economic Identification of Social Classes* (London: Routledge & Kegan Paul).

Carver, Terrell (1975), *Karl Marx: Texts on Method* (Oxford: Basil Blackwell).

Cohen, Stephen (1974), *Bukharin and the Bolshevik Revolution: A Political Biography, 1888–1938* (London: Wildwood House).

Collins, Randall (1980), 'Weber's last theory of capitalism: a systematization', *American Sociological Review*, vol. 45, no. 6 (1980) pp. 925–42.

Engels, Friedrich (1844), 'Umrisse zu einer Kritik der politischen Ökonomie', *Deutsch-Französische Jahrbücher*.

Fine, Ben and Harris, Laurence (1979), *Rereading 'Capital'* (London: Macmillan).

Fleischmann, E. (1964), 'De Weber à Nietzsche', *Archives Européennes de Sociologie*, V (1964) pp. 190–238.

Freeman, Christopher (ed.) (1983), *Long Waves in the World Economy* (London: Butterworth).

Friedmann, Milton (1962), *Capitalism and Freedom* (Chicago: University of Chicago Press).

Gay, Peter (1952), *The Dilemma of Democratic Socialism: Eduard Bernstein's Challenge to Marx* (New York: Columbia University Press).

Godelier, Maurice (1972), 'Structure and contradiction in *Capital*', in Robin Blackburn (ed.), *Ideology in Social Science* (London: Fontana/Collins).

Green, Robert W. (ed.) (1959), *Protestantism and Capitalism: The Weber Thesis and Its Critics* (Boston: D. C. Heath & Co.).

Habermas, Jürgen (1976), *Legitimation Crisis* (London: Heinemann).

Hardach, Gerd, and Karras, Dieter (1978), *A Short History of Socialist Economic Thought* (London: Edward Arnold).

Harvey, David (1982), *The Limits to Capital* (Oxford: Basil Blackwell).

Hayek, F. A. (1944), *The Road to Serfdom* (London: Routledge & Sons).

Hayek, F. A. (1949), *Individualism and Economic Order* (London: Routledge & Kegan Paul).

Hayek, F. A. (ed.) (1954) *Capitalism and the Historians* (London: Routledge & Kegan Paul).

Hayek, F. A. (1982), *Law, Legislation and Liberty* (3 vols in 1) (London: Routledge & Kegan Paul).

Heertje, Arnold (ed.) (1981), *Schumpeter's Vision: 'Capitalism, Socialism and Democracy' after 40 years* (New York and Eastbourne: Praeger Publishers).

Hegedüs, András (1976), *Socialism and Bureaucracy* (London: Allison & Busby).

Hilferding, Rudolf (1910) *Finance Capital: A Study of the Latest Phase of Capitalist Development* (London: Routledge & Kegan Paul, 1981).

Hilferding, Rudolf (1915), 'Arbeitsgemeinschaft der Klassen?', *Der Kampf*, 8 (1915).

Hilferding, Rudolf (1924a), 'Probleme der Zeit', *Die Gesellschaft*, 1 (1924).

Hilferding, Rudolf (1924b), 'Realistischer Pazifismus', *Die Gesellschaft*, 1 (1924).

Hilferding, Rudolf (1927), 'Die Aufgaben der Sozialdemokratie in der Republik' (published speech, Berlin 1927. English trans. of part in Bottomore and Goode, 1983).

Hilferding, Rudolf (1940), 'State capitalism or totalitarian state economy', *Socialist Courier* (1940) (repr. in *Modern Review*, 1, 1947).

Hilferding, Rudolf (1941), *Das historische Problem*, unfinished work, first published in *Zeitschrift für Politik* (new series) 1, (1954): English trans. of part in Bottomore, 1981.

Hughes, H. Stuart (1958), *Consciousness and Society* (New York: Alfred A. Knopf).

Hutchinson, T. W. (1981), *The Politics and Philosophy of Economics: Marxians, Keynesians and Austrians* (Oxford: Basil Blackwell).

Jessop, Bob (1982), *The Capitalist State* (Oxford: Martin Robertson).

Kautsky, Karl (1899), *Bernstein und das sozialdemokratische Programm* (Stuttgart: J. H. W. Dietz).

Kautsky, Karl (1901–2), 'Krisentheorien', *Die Neue Zeit*, 20, 2 (1901–2) pp. 37–47, 76–81, 110–18, 133–43.

Konrád, George, and Szelényi, Ivan (1979), *The Intellectuals on the Road to Class Power* (Brighton: Harvester Press).

Kühne, Karl (1979), *Economics and Marxism* (2 vols) (London: Macmillan).

Kumar, Krishan (1983), 'Pre-capitalist and non-capitalist factors in the development of capitalism: Fred Hirsch and Joseph Schumpeter', in Adrian Ellis and Krishan Kumar (eds), *Dilemmas of Liberal Democracies* (London and New York: Tavistock Publications).

Lasswell, Harold D., and Lerner, Daniel (1965), *World Revolutionary Elites: Studies in Coercive Ideological Movements* (Cambridge, Mass.: MIT Press).

Lederer, Emil (1912), *Die Privatangestellten in der modernen Wirtschaftsentwicklung* (Tübingen: J. C. B. Mohr).

Lenin, V. I. (1916), *Imperialism, the Highest Stage of Capitalism*, in *Collected Works*, Vol. 22 (Moscow: Progress Publishers, 1964).

Löwith, Karl (1932), *Max Weber and Karl Marx* (London: Allen & Unwin, 1982).

Lukács, György (1971), 'Prefatory note' to István Mészáros (ed.), *Aspects of History and Class Consciousness* (London: Routledge & Kegan Paul).

Lukes, Steven (1973), *Individualism* (Oxford: Basil Blackwell).

Macfarlane, Alan (1978), *The Origins of English Individualism* (Oxford: Basil Blackwell).

Machajski, Waclaw (1905), *The Intellectual Worker*. In Russian. His argument is summarized in Nomad, 1959, pp. 96–117.

McLellan, David (ed.) (1983), *Marx: The First Hundred Years* (London: Fontana).

Maddison, Angus (1982), *Phases of Capitalist Development* (Oxford and New York: Oxford University Press).

Mandel, Ernest (1975), *Late Capitalism* (London: New Left Books).

Marshall, Gordon (1980), *Presbyteries and Profits: Calvinism and the Development of Capitalism in Scotland, 1560–1707* (Oxford: Clarendon Press).

Marshall, Gordon (1982), *In Search of the Spirit of Capitalism: An Essay on Max Weber's Protestant Ethic Thesis* (London: Hutchinson).

Marx, Karl (1844), *Economic and Philosophical Manuscripts* (first published 1932).

Marx, Karl (1847), *The Poverty of Philosophy*.

Marx, Karl (1852), *The Eighteenth Brumaire of Louis Bonaparte*.

Marx, Karl (1857–8), *Grundrisse* (first published 1939–41) (Harmondsworth: Penguin Books, 1973).

Marx, Karl (1859), *A Contribution to the Critique of Political Economy*.

Marx, Karl (1861–79), *Theories of Surplus Value* (first published 1905–10).

Marx, Karl (1867, 1885, 1894), *Capital* (3 vols).

Marx, Karl, and Engels, Friedrich (1845–6), *The German Ideology* (first published 1932).

Marx, Karl, and Engels, Friedrich (1848), *Communist Manifesto*.

Mommsen, Wolfgang J. (1959), *Max Weber und die deutsche Politik 1890–1920* (Tübingen: J. C. B. Mohr).

Mommsen, Wolfgang J. (1974), *The Age of Bureaucracy: Perspectives on the Political Sociology of Max Weber* (Oxford: Basil Blackwell).

Neumann, Franz (1944), *Behemoth: The Structure and Practice of National Socialism*, 2nd edn (New York: Oxford University Press).

Nomad, Max (1959), *Aspects of Revolt* (New York: Bookman Associates).

Panitch, L. (1980), 'Recent Theorizations of Corporatism', *British Journal of Sociology*, 31 (1980).

Parkin, Frank (1982), *Max Weber* (Chichester and London: Ellis Horwood/Tavistock).

Popper, Karl (1945), *The Open Society and Its Enemies* (London: George Routledge & Sons).

Popper, Karl (1957), *The Poverty of Historicism* (London: Routledge & Kegan Paul).

Poulantzas, Nicos (1973), *Political Power and Social Classes* (London: New Left Books).

Poulantzas, Nicos (1975), *Classes in Contemporary Capitalism* (London: New Left Books).

Przeworski, Adam (1977), 'Proletariat into a class: the process of class formation from Karl Kautsky's *The Class Struggle* to recent controversies', *Politics and Society*, vol. 7, no. 4 (1977).

Renner, Karl (1916), 'Probleme des Marxismus', *Der Kampf*, 9 (English trans. of part in Bottomore and Goode, 1978).

Renner, Karl (1953), *Wandlungen der modernen Gesellschaft* (Vienna: Wiener Volksbuchhandlung).

Robinson, Joan (1942), *An Essay on Marxian Economics* (London: Macmillan).

Routh, Guy (1980), *Occupation and Pay in Great Britain 1906–79* (London: Macmillan).

Schumpeter, J. A. (1911), *The Theory of Economic Development* revised edn 1926 (Cambridge, Mass.: Harvard University Press, 1934).

Schumpeter, J. A. (1919), 'The sociology of imperialisms', in Paul Sweezy (ed.), *Imperialism and Social Classes* (New York: Augustus M. Kelley, 1951).

Schumpeter, J. A. (1927), 'Social classes in an ethnically homogeneous environment', in Paul Sweezy (ed.), *Imperialism and Social Classes* (New York: Augustus M. Kelley, 1951).

Schumpeter, J. A. (1928), 'The instability of capitalism', *Economic Journal*, 38 (September 1928).

Schumpeter, J. A. (1939), *Business Cycles* (2 vols) (New York: McGraw-Hill).

Schumpeter, J. A. (1942), *Capitalism, Socialism and Democracy*, 5th edn (London: Allen & Unwin, 1976).

Schumpeter, J. A. (1954), *History of Economic Analysis* (New York: Oxford University Press).

Smith, Adam (1759), *The Theory of Moral Sentiments* (London).

Smith, Adam (1776), *The Wealth of Nations* (London).

Smithies, A. (1951), 'Memorial: Joseph Alois Schumpeter, 1883–1950', in S. E. Harris (ed.) *Schumpeter: Social Scientist* (Cambridge, Mass.: Harvard University Press).

Sombart, Werner (1902), *Der moderne Kapitalismus: Historisch-systematische Darstellung des gesamteuropäischen Wirtschaftslebens von seinen Anfängen bis zur Gegenwart* (3 vols) (Munich and Leipzig: Duncker & Humblot, 1902; 2nd edn 1924–7).

Sombart, Werner (1906), *Why is there no Socialism in the United States?* (London: Macmillan, 1976).

Sweezy, Paul (1942), *The Theory of Capitalist Development* (New York: Oxford University Press).

Sweezy, Paul (1972), *Modern Capitalism and Other Essays* (New York and London: Monthly Review Press).

Tawney, R. H. (1952), *Equality*, 4th revised edn (London: Allen & Unwin).

Tilly, Charles (ed.) (1975), *The Formation of National States in Western Europe* (Princeton: Princeton University Press, 1975).

Touraine, Alain (1965), *Sociologie de l'action* (Paris: Éditions du Seuil).

Touraine, Alain (1971), *The Post-Industrial Society* (New York: Random House).

Touraine, Alain (1977), *The Self-Production of Society* (Chicago: University of Chicago Press).

Touraine, Alain (1980), *L'Après-Socialisme* (Paris: Bernard Grasset).

Tsuru, Shigeto (ed.) (1961), *Has Capitalism Changed?* (Tokyo: Iwanami Shoten).

Uno, Kozo (1980), *Principles of Political Economy: Theory of a Purely Capitalist Society* (Brighton: Harvester Press).

Weber, Max (1895), 'Der Nationalstaat und die Wirtschaftspolitik', inaugural lecture, published in *Gesammelte Politische Schriften*, 3rd edn (Tübingen: J. C. B. Mohr, 1971).

Weber, Max (1904–5), *The Protestant Ethic and the Spirit of Capitalism* (London: Allen & Unwin, 1976).

Weber, Max (1918a), *Parliament and Government in a Reconstructed Germany* (English trans. as appendix to *Economy and Society*, Vol. 3).

Weber, Max (1918b), 'Socialism' (lecture, published in *Gesammelte Aufsätze zur Soziologie und Sozialpolitik* (1924). In J. E. T. Eldridge (ed.), *Max Weber: The Interpretation of Social Reality* (London: Michael Joseph, 1970), pp. 191–219.

Weber, Max (1921), *Economy and Society* (3 vols) (New York: Bedminster Press, 1968).

Weber, Max (1923), *General Economic History* (New York: Collier Books, 1961).

Wirth, Margaret (1972), *Kapitalismustheorie in der DDR: Entstehung und Entwicklung der Theorie des staatsmonopolistischen Kapitalismus* (Frankfurt: Suhrkamp).

Wright, Erik Olin (1978), *Class, Crises and the State* (London: New Left Books).

Wright, G. H. von (1971), *Explanation and Understanding* (London: Routledge & Kegan Paul).

Index

Index